PUBLISHER: Amy Marson

CREATIVE DIRECTOR: Gailen Runge

ART DIRECTOR/BOOK DESIGNER:
Kristy Zacharias

EDITOR: S. Michele Fry

TECHNICAL EDITORS: Helen Frost
and Amanda Siegfried

PRODUCTION COORDINATOR:
Jenny Davis

PRODUCTION EDITOR:
Alice Mace Nakanishi

ILLUSTRATOR: Jenny Davis

PHOTO ASSISTANT:
Mary Peyton Peppo

PHOTOGRAPHY BY
Nissa Brehmer and Diane Pedersen
of C&T Publishing, Inc., unless
otherwise noted

Published by Stash Books, an imprint of C&T Publishing, Inc., P.O. Box 1456,
Lafayette, CA 94549

Library of Congress Cataloging-in-Publication Data
Conner, Lindsay, 1983-
 Modern bee : 13 quilts to make with friends / Lindsay Conner.
     pages cm
 ISBN 978-1-60705-730-7 (soft cover)
 1. Patchwork--Patterns. 2. Quilting--Patterns. I. Title.
 TT835.C6494 2013
 746.46--dc23

                              2013011954

Printed in China

10 9 8 7 6 5 4 3 2 1

C-1

modern
Bee

13 QUILTS TO MAKE WITH FRIENDS

LINDSAY CONNER

an imprint of C&T Publishing

Dedication

This book is dedicated to my family. Mom, you bought me my first sewing machine, even when I didn't think I would want one, and dragged me along with you to craft stores nearly every week when I was growing up. I wouldn't be where I am today without your creative influences. Dad, you've always been an example to me of what it means to work hard and put myself toward something. I am forever grateful for the path you've provided and your sacrifices for our family. And my husband, Matt, thank you for allowing me the space to create. I couldn't have a better support system than a spouse who truly believes in me … and puts up with my reality TV habit.

Acknowledgments

To the team at C&T, you have brought my idea to life and I am forever grateful for your dedication, editorial and creative direction, and friendship. Many thanks to Coats & Clark, The Electric Quilt Company, FreeSpirit Fabrics, Olfa, Pellon, and Timeless Treasures for generously providing materials to make the quilts in this book. Thank you to the Indianapolis Modern Quilt Guild and the ladies of Mod Stitches for contributing to the *String Circles* charity quilt: Val Campbell, Cyndi Clayton, Katie Clayton, Gretchen Fisher, Amy Garro, Rachael Adele Heger, Jessica Kelly, Lindsay Lefevere, Colleen Molen, Tisha Nagel, Elizabeth Rea, Jenny Shamblin, and Cindy Wiens. And to the Mod Stitches bee, this book would not be possible without your awesome creativity, attention to detail, and willingness to journey with me in this project.

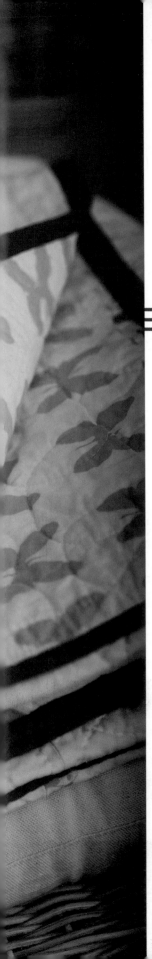

Contents

Introduction

The Need to Create

I was a cubicle dweller who needed a creative outlet for my nights and weekends. Like so many people, I was looking for a way to create. Between days spent staring at a screen and plenty of nights spent looking at some other screen, I was feeling a little … uninspired.

One afternoon several years ago, I answered a phone call from my mom, who was shopping for deals—something she taught me to do quite well. "Lindsay, I found a Hello Kitty sewing machine on clearance—half off! It's so cute. Do you want it, maybe for your birthday?" I wasn't sure, to be honest. I'd never used a sewing machine, and it seemed to fall into the *want* rather than *need* category. But for the cute factor alone, I obliged my mom's request to buy me the sewing machine as an early birthday gift.

In just a few months, I lived and breathed sewing and quilting. It wasn't long until I found an online world of people just like me. In one year, I somehow managed to sign up for fifteen craft swaps (an arrangement by two or more people to exchange crafts by mail). Looking back, my postage bill that year was huge. But the act of crafting for others helped me to grow in my sewing skills and connect with others like me. It's an investment of time and money that I would repeat any day.

Soon after I discovered the online sewing world, I started meeting quilters in person. I joined the Indianapolis Modern Quilt Guild (my local guild at the time) and then convinced my husband to go away for the weekend so I could host a quilting retreat for a dozen women at our house. It was life-giving to meet other quilters from my area. Would you believe that two of them actually worked right down the hall from me? With Lindsay, my namesake, and Elizabeth at the office, I began to look forward to quilting show-and-tell at work, swaps, and fabric-sale alerts. One day we even ordered 61 yards of Flea Market Fancy and held a fabric-cutting party in a spare conference room.

Meeting with other quilters, whether in person or online, kept me motivated and creatively charged. I soon got to the point where I always had a new project in mind. When I traveled to new places, I started seeing quilt motifs in the sidewalks, on street signs, and in architecture. The ideas wouldn't leave me alone, and I sometimes woke up in the middle of the night with designs for a new sewing project.

When a local friend asked if I'd like to join my first online quilting bee, I asked, "What's that?" She explained that a bee was like a craft swap, with a group of twelve people who make and swap quilt blocks. Each month of the year, one person would choose the block design for everyone to make, and then all members would mail the requested blocks back to that person. At the time, I wasn't sure if I had the quilting prowess to join a bee, but I was curious enough to try it. Overall, it was a great experience to learn some new techniques and also get to know some local quilters.

Over the next few years, I joined several online quilting bees, swapping patchwork blocks with quilters across the country. In 2011, an online friend, Elizabeth, invited me to join a virtual quilting bee she was putting together. I'd first met Elizabeth through reading her blog—we got to know each other better when I made her a messenger bag as part of a swap. Did I have time to join another bee and commit for a whole year? That was debatable, but I decided to join anyway.

We called the bee "Mod Stitches." The talent and creativity within the group was so strong—these were some of the most inspiring quilting bloggers I had met. All the members of the group met first through our blogs or through Flickr, and we organized the bee as a Flickr group so we could share photos, block instructions, and the bee's mailing schedule in one central place.

Thanks to our blogs and social media, we got to share a bit of our lives, too. I am among the first to know when my friends send their little ones off to school or find a mailbox stuffed with "happy mail," including an enviable stack of new fabric. Many of the quilters I've met online are people I get to meet in person at sewing and quilting events across the country. Among them are some of my closest friends—the people I know I can count on to share my greatest joys and biggest disappointments.

Megan Bohr
PAINTER'S PALETTE, page 48

Photo by Michael Hanna

Photo by Lindsey Bohr

Jeni Baker
STACKED WINDMILLS, page 61

Katie Bowlby
CORDELIA'S GARDEN, page 66

Photo by Ashley Leath

Jessica Kelly
TRELLIS CROSSROADS, page 78

Elizabeth Dackson
COME TOGETHER, page 56

Photo by Jesse Tendler

Photo by Jason Kelly

Cindy Wiens
NEON NINJA STAR, page 71

Photo by Christa Wiens

THE *Mod Stitches Bee*

Lindsay Conner
BASEBALL CURVES, page 90,
and STRING CIRCLES, page 104

Jennifer Mathis
PLAYING CARDS, page 38

Amy (Sukie) Newbold
MOSAIC TILES, page 32

Photo by James Mathis

Photo by Jeremiah Blackford

Photo by Brad Newbold

Photo by Brad Molen

Colleen Molen
ZIGGY STARDUST, page 84

Photo by Adrianne Ove

Adrianne Ove
BLUEBELL'S CABIN, page 43

Elena Roscoe
TRIPLE STAR, page 98

Photo by Jemma Coleman

Let's Make a Book!

The quilt patterns in this book are crafted with a modern aesthetic by the Mod Stitches bee. Our designs are inspired by everything from traditional quilt blocks to doodles to bits and pieces of everyday life. Katie's design (pages 11 and 66) is a modern version of her grandmother's quilt, a family heirloom (below left), while Cindy found the inspiration for her quilt (page 71) from a booth at a fast-food restaurant.

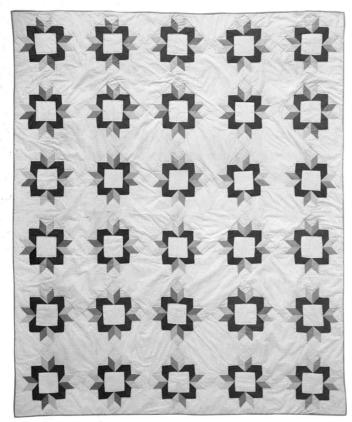

The patterns in this book are organized by skill level—beginner, confident beginner, and intermediate. By quilting along with the book from January to December, or following any method that works for you, you will have mastered skills ranging from piecing squares and triangles to sewing more advanced block-in-block designs with tiny piecing. Each of the thirteen projects includes block instructions as well as a pattern to finish a quilt.

The quilts can be completed in sequence or out of order—with a bee or on your own. If you are sewing with a group, the book shares tips on mailing bee blocks (page 18) and fixing returned blocks (page 22) as well as giving you the fabric requirements needed for each bee member with each project. At the end of the book, you'll also find some quilting basics to help you finish your quilt—how to baste, assemble, bind, and more.

Modern Bee—13 Quilts to Make with Friends

Bee. Keeping

Starting a Bee

Quilting bees began as a way for people to socialize around a common hobby. Of course, there's the added efficiency of sewing together in a group—you can finish an entire quilt in a fraction of the time. But more importantly, sewing with others is a way to creatively stretch yourself. For example, you will sew with fabric and shapes that you would not have chosen, and chances are you will have to learn something that's outside of your comfort zone. On the plus side, you'll have the support of the bee when you have questions.

But how do you find a quilting bee? Where do all of these people hang out? One place to start is to get involved with a local quilt guild and see if any bees exist. To find a quilting bee online, I recommend joining Flickr and visiting the group Quilting Bee Blocks.

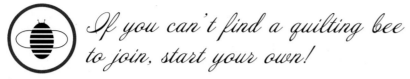

If you can't find a quilting bee to join, start your own!

Still, it's a good idea to be a participant in a bee before organizing one yourself. That way, you'll know what to expect and can help the group run smoothly. The point person and organizer will need to do a few things for the bee:

1. CHOOSE A FORUM

Join Flickr (flickr.com), Quilting Board (quiltingboard.com), or Swap-bot (swap-bot.com) to find open bees and swaps online. A local quilting group may also be a place to form a bee.

TIP: You can reach out to others who follow or write quilting blogs and see whether they know of any bees accepting new members. Perhaps they'd like to join with you in starting a bee.

2. RECRUIT MEMBERS

Take an email address, phone number, and mailing address for each member. Print out a master list and stay on top of changes like a new address or phone number during the bee.

TIP: When starting a new bee, you may wish to check the bee or swap history of incoming members. For instance, do they have an active blog or Flickr account? Do they tend to over-commit or send late? If you do some research and find that they have caused problems for other online swaps or bees, you can ask them to explain any issues.

3. SET THE RULES

How long will the bee last and how many blocks will each person sew? What types of blocks or fabric are acceptable?

TIP: Expectations are very important to communicate when starting a bee. Consider taking a break during busy months like mid-summer or December, when bee members are likely to have other commitments. This could make it less likely that members will flake or bail out during busy seasons.

4. KEEP TABS

Keep track of those who have sent or received blocks each month. Contact members who are not meeting the deadlines or communicating regularly. Find solutions if blocks are lost in the mail.

TIP: The bee organizer may want to create *angel blocks* for members who do not receive their finished blocks. These are extra blocks in the person's chosen fabric and style that will replace lost or never-received blocks.

Other Types of Bees

For a spin on the traditional twelve-month, twelve-member quilting bee, consider switching up the rules to fit you and your group.

SPECIFIC BLOCK SWAP

Choose one style of block in specified colors, and invite people to make as many as they'd like. They can send the blocks to a central location and will receive back the same number of blocks made by others in the bee. For example, you could ask for Flying Geese blocks in shades of red and blue. This is a great way to maximize the variety of prints in a quilt without shopping for more fabric.

SIX-MONTH BEE

Do you have commitment phobia? Consider a shorter time frame. To organize a six-month bee, invite twelve quilters to double up on assigned months (January through June, for example). Each quilter makes two blocks per month, including one for her own quilt.

SAMPLER BEE

Form a group of four to six bee members, and ask each person to choose a color combination (such as yellow, aqua, and gray) for her quilt blocks. A photo mosaic is a helpful tool for sharing colors. Working from your stash, make the same block for each member of the group in her chosen colors by the end of the swap. Each member can choose the block she'd like to make. It's a good idea to check with the group to make sure two people don't make the same block pattern. Three to six months is a good time frame, and it's easy to repeat for those who'd like to join again for the next session.

At the end of the bee, you'll have a sampler quilt (many styles of blocks) in your chosen colors.

I joined the Flickr group 4x5 Modern Quilt Bee, a modern sampler bee that included about 100 members in more than a dozen different "hives" (smaller groups). In a hive with four to six members, you can repeat the bee until each person has enough blocks to make a full-size quilt. As a part of this bee, I participated in three rounds (organized by seasons of the year) and collected fifteen blocks total. Because the bee alternated members each season, it was a great way to collect blocks in a variety of styles while getting to know five new quilters each round.

ROUND-ROBIN BEE

To start a round-robin bee, each quilter comes up with a theme and makes one block or row for her own quilt. She mails this to the next person in the bee, who adds a row or block inspired by that person's design and colors. The next month, that person mails the two blocks to the third person on the list (think of *The Sisterhood of the Traveling Pants*). At any given point in time, someone else in the bee is adding to your quilt while you are adding to someone else's. When you finally see the finished quilt, it has been out of your hands for a year and comes back to you with a treasury of different designs and styles.

MOD BEGINNINGS

Some people fall into sewing by chance, and others come from a long line of quilters. How did you start quilting?

I started quilting shortly after moving into my first apartment in 2009. I had my heart set on making a quilt, and after that first one, I was completely hooked! —JENI BAKER

I bought my first sewing machine back in 2010. Little did I know I was on a road that would totally change my life. I've absolutely fallen head over heels with quilting over the years, after having taught myself from library books and blogs, and I cannot imagine my life without it. —ELIZABETH DACKSON

I started quilting when I began sewing in 2010. I was pregnant with my second child and came across a tutorial for a patchwork baby quilt and decided to give it a try. It was instant love, and I've been sewing and quilting ever since. —JENNIFER MATHIS

I began sewing when I was about five years old. I watched my mother make all sorts of things on her Kenmore machine, so she showed me how to make dresses for my Barbie dolls. I was allowed to sew only by hand at first, so later when she allowed me to actually sit at her machine, I felt very special. I made the transition to quilting just a few years ago after signing up for a quilt class on a whim. I enjoyed formulating the perfect fabric combination and then watching it come to life. I was quite giddy and actually jumped up and down when I saw my first quilt top completely pieced. —ELENA ROSCOE

Choosing a Block and Fabric

For the Mod Stitches bee, we assigned each person a month to be the host. One of the most fun parts of a quilting bee is choosing a block pattern and fabric for your month. When writing the block instructions and deciding how much fabric to send in the mail, it's a good idea to make a test block yourself and take notes on how much fabric you use. Jot down details, such as which way to press the seams and if the quilters should trim the block. Keep in mind that you'll want to choose a pattern that loosely matches the skill level of the quilters in your group, while still challenging them to try something new.

If you are providing the fabric for your bee, you can cut an assortment for each person that's a little more than you think they'll need. Some quilters suggest sending the equivalent of 1½ fat quarters to each bee member. Let the bee members know if you'd like them to send fabric scraps back to you with the finished block.

If it's a bee where members sew from their own fabric stash, you won't need to send any fabric. But you should still send instructions to specify what colors or fabric designs you like.

Mailing Fabric

TIPS FOR THE HOST

When participating in a quilting bee, each person gets the chance to be both the *host*, who sends fabric and writes the block instructions, and the *recipient*, who makes the requested block and returns it in the mail to the host. Here are some helpful tips for sending fabric and receiving quilt blocks in the mail:

1. Place the fabric in a zipper-sealed plastic bag to be mailed in an envelope (6″ × 9″ manila envelopes work well). The plastic bag is protection in case the envelope gets wet. If you are reusing an envelope, make sure to cross out the previous address thoroughly or cover it with a new mailing label.

2. Insert a note, "If this package is lost or stolen, please return to: [name and address]." Place the note in the plastic bag and make sure it is visible. If the fabric or completed block slips out of the envelope en route, it stands a greater chance of getting safely returned to that month's host.

3. Include printed block instructions or post them online. It doesn't hurt to do both. State the completed block size, how many blocks you'd like the recipients to make if more than one, and if they should send back fabric scraps. Let bee members know if you would like the block to be trimmed or if you'd prefer to do the trimming.

4. Keep a list of blocks you've received and send a thank-you note. Keep your bee organizer in the loop if you don't receive blocks by the deadline.

TIPS FOR THE RECIPIENT

1. Consider including a hand-written note or business card with your sewn bee blocks. You can also jot down the name of the bee (in case the recipient is in more than one bee) on the envelope or an index card.

2. Mail blocks by the due date. As a courtesy, let the host know if your block will be late. For extra security and peace of mind when mailing bee blocks, you may wish to add delivery confirmation or insurance.

3. Place the block in a zipper-sealed plastic bag. Include the note the host sent that says where the package should be returned if lost.

4. Let the host know when you've mailed the block to her.

Notes and cards received with completed blocks

WHY DO YOU QUILT?

Any hobby, from running marathons to sustainable gardening, has its champions—the people who truly "get it." So what's to love about quilting?

When I first got into the sewing/quilting hobby, it was a way to occupy my time without socializing with other people. I mean, I had a handful of friends and none of them were really into quilting. As more time passed, I began to make more and more friends because of my hobby. My creations inspired not only people around me but others in the sewing community. —SUKIE NEWBOLD

Sewing and quilting has really become my favorite way to express my creativity. I love being able to take fabric and turn it into something completely personalized and unique, whether a quilt, a new bag, or a gift for friends or family. —JESSICA KELLY

Quilting gives me a chance to express myself in a way that helps me to branch out and try new techniques, yet strengthens my ties to the past. It also has been a source of "therapy" through some hard times. —CINDY WIENS

For me, quilting connects me to my family and my past. I come from a long line of sewists, and I love having this connection with them. There's nothing better than making a handmade gift for a loved one. —KATIE BOWLBY

My sewing and quilting time is my "me time." It's the time that I spend where I turn off everything else and really just let myself create, which is a wonderful feeling. —ELIZABETH DACKSON

Making a Block:
Tips for the Recipient

It's your turn to make a block for someone else. Here are some details to keep in mind:

1. When opening fabric from a bee member, take a quick note of the pieces the host included and write down the measurements as needed. If you are missing any pieces, contact that month's host and see if you can substitute fabric from your stash or if she'd prefer to mail you the missing fabric.

2. Follow the host's block instructions, asking any questions you have before you start sewing. Be sure you have key information such as the block size (usually the unfinished size, but double-check) and how she prefers the seams to be pressed.

3. Take a photo of your completed block. If you have a group set up online, sharing your block photos is a great way to build camaraderie in the group and to let members know when a block is in the mail.

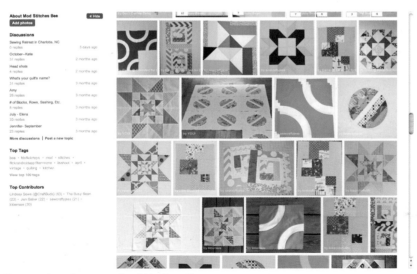

Bee members share completed blocks online.

Bee Troubleshooting and Common Problems

Even with the most explicit instructions, sometimes sewing with others is a challenge. Though you may have to make some fixes after the fact, many of these issues can be avoided with a little advance planning and clear communication.

1. SOMEONE USED THE WRONG FABRIC

If sewing with fabric from each quilter's own stash, the colors, prints, and quality may be way off from what you asked for. And if you sent bee members fabric to use, there's always the chance that someone will try to sneak in another print—or do so by mistake.

 Mod fixes:

- **THE COLORS ARE ALL WRONG.**   Before swapping blocks, ask each bee member to create a photo mosaic of fabrics or images that she'd like to use as her color palette (such as yellow, aqua, and gray). You can upload mosaics to a site such as Flickr or post on a central blog. *Aqua* can mean totally different things to different people, so encourage bee members to ask about color preferences before making their blocks, if in doubt.

Color palette

When in doubt on color choices, share a photo of your fabrics with the bee before sewing together the block.

- **THE PRINTS ARE A STYLE I DON'T LIKE**
To avoid undesirable prints, the host of a bee can list the names of preferred fabric designers. If bee members have questions about whether a specific fabric works, ask them to post a photo or link to the fabric, and the bee can give feedback. You don't have to be the fabric police, but if most of the bee agrees that they do not like batiks, then don't use batiks. You will probably see stronger interest in sticking with the bee if the members like the fabrics they are working with, so advise the group to steer clear of unpopular fabrics.

- **THE FABRIC IS LOW QUALITY** Blocks sewn with thin, low-quality fabrics can look quite odd next to the other blocks that all seem to match. Most bees I participate in specify that the fabric should be of "quilt-store quality." As a general rule, this means that the fabric comes from either a quilt shop or a national chain store carrying high-quality designer quilting fabrics. For example, I once made a quilt block with a mix of fabrics from different stores. When I held the block up to the light, I could tell that the vintage sheeting fabric and chain-store fabric were more transparent than the others. High-quality fabrics are less likely to bleed in the wash and are usually more durable. Some bees also allow specialty fabrics like vintage sheets. If there's any doubt on fabric quality, it's a good idea to run the question by your bee!

If the host didn't send enough fabric, ask if it's okay to send a partial block for her to complete.

- **IS THAT *YOUR* FABRIC IN THERE?** When providing the fabric for bee members to use in the blocks, let them know when you are mailing the package, how to correctly use the fabrics, and whether it is okay for them to add any of their own fabric. You may feel like you are over-explaining, but quilt bee newbies will appreciate hearing your expectations. If someone adds a random piece of fabric against your wishes, a crafty solution might be to appliqué another fabric over the wrong one. You could also consider working that block into the back of the quilt. One quilting blogger confesses to making hot pads from wonky blocks that don't fit her quilt design.

- **I DIDN'T RECEIVE ENOUGH FABRIC**
Contact the host of that month's block. She may choose to send you more fabric or she may approve the use of fabric from your stash. Send her a picture of what you're considering. During Colleen's month, I was short some solid fabric, so she agreed that I could send her my nearly finished blocks and she would add the extra cream fabric.

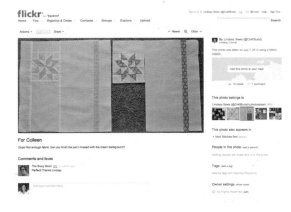

2. THE BLOCKS I RECEIVED AREN'T SEWN CORRECTLY

Poor construction or overzealous trimming of blocks can be a real downer. But you might be able to creatively avoid this problem or salvage the poorly sewn blocks.

Construction oopsies

 *Mod fixes:*

- **YOU ASKED FOR A BLOCK WITH A STAR IN THE CENTER, BUT ALL YOU SEE IS A BIG WRINKLE WHERE POINTS TOUCH** Consider ripping out the offending stitches and trying them again, or relocate the block to the back of the quilt, where it won't be a focal point. A creative use of appliqué (like a fabric yo-yo or patch) on the finished quilt could be another solution.

- **YOU SPECIFIED THAT BLOCKS SHOULD BE LEFT UNTRIMMED, BUT SOMEONE CUT HER BLOCK BEFORE MAILING** Now it's too small, and it's lopsided. If the block has a border, see if you can rip out the stitches and reattach one or two sides (with a narrower seam allowance) to lengthen the block. If the block cannot be fixed, politely let the bee member know that you couldn't use the too-small block. You can ask her to make another one or you might have to make a replacement.

- **YOU ASKED FOR SEAMS TO BE PRESSED OPEN OR TO THE DARK SIDE, BUT YOU RECEIVED BLOCKS THAT LOOK LIKE THEY WERE NOT PRESSED AT ALL** Many times, you can sneak into that block with a pair of pointy scissors and snip the stitches to press the already-sewn seams to the correct side. You may want to provide feedback to the bee member who didn't follow the directions to save other months' hosts from running into similar trouble and to keep the bee member from getting a bad reputation.

- **INSTEAD OF HAVING A ¼″ SEAM ALLOWANCE, THE SEAMS ARE NEARLY COMING APART** Or, the seam allowance is too wide, so the finished block is too small. If the seam allowances are too small, you may be able to take apart half or more of the block and then reinforce each section with a scant ¼″ seam before reassembling. Seams that are too narrow will probably have to be picked out, or the entire block trimmed smaller if it will not be noticeable in the finished quilt. Although it may be an awkward conversation, letting a bee member know about any unusable blocks will help save others from facing the same issue.

3. I NEVER RECEIVED MY BLOCK IN THE MAIL

When you go to the trouble of sending out fabric to your bee members only to never see it again, it's a sad situation. By being proactive, you can help alleviate this problem.

 Mod fixes:

- **A BEE MEMBER DID NOT SEND YOUR BLOCK AT ALL, AND NOW SHE WON'T EVEN RETURN YOUR EMAILS**   One of the keys to avoiding this problem is to be very clear in your expectations for the bee. From the very beginning, let everyone know the deadlines for sending out fabric, returning finished blocks, and any other pertinent dates. Remind bee members about two weeks before blocks are due. From the beginning, you can set an expectation that if anyone is unable to meet a deadline, she will need to return the fabric to the host. Everyone gets busy at times, so you might want to give a grace period of two weeks from the deadline. Having an active bee host who is highly organized generally helps increase bee participation across the board!

  If the expectations were clear but you still haven't received your block, try messaging the bee member and ask if she will be able to complete it. If not, politely ask if she can return your fabric so you can make the block. It's often a good idea to buy a little more fabric than you will need when sewing with a bee, just in case you can't get the fabric back from someone.

- **A BEE MEMBER SAYS SHE'S MAILED YOUR BLOCK, BUT YOU STILL HAVEN'T RECEIVED IT**   To keep this from happening, ask each bee member to post a photograph of her block online before she mails it. (Then you know it's really finished!) Ask her to add delivery confirmation and send you the tracking number so you can track the block's delivery. If a particular bee member always forgets to photograph her block and bee members complain that they are not receiving blocks from this person, she may need to leave the bee.

- **HAVE AN ANGEL BLOCK SYSTEM**
  It helps to have a plan in place for blocks that go missing in action. Some bees like to have a volunteer each month make angel blocks. These are quilt blocks made specifically for a host who does not receive a block for one reason or another, for which the maker expects nothing in return. If you're planning to make angel blocks for a bee member, it's best to wait until you are pretty sure that the host will not be receiving the promised blocks. If she receives the original block late plus the extra angel block, perhaps she can be encouraged to return the favor by making an angel block for someone else down the line.

4. MY BEE IS A BAD FIT FOR ME

Whether from a lack of interaction, dissimilar personalities, or varying skill levels among bee members, you might end up in a bee that you wish you hadn't joined.

 Mod fixes:

- **THE QUILTERS IN YOUR BEE DON'T SEEM VERY CHATTY** You've posted your life story to the message board, but everyone else seems to be disinterested. Try to get to know the members of the group before signing up or in the first few weeks of the bee. Ask them questions about their lives and introduce yourself, but try to be realistic about your expectations. It takes time to get to know a group of crafters, and some people may be juggling several bees at a time, not to mention life's other concerns. (Yes, some people think there's more to life than quilting!)

- **YOU ARE NEW TO QUILTING AND THE REQUIRED BLOCKS ARE TOO COMPLEX** One of the benefits of joining a quilting bee is the chance to learn new skills and techniques, so keep an open mind when someone wants you to try a paper-pieced block or sew with curves. Practice elements of the block with fabric scraps or watch a video tutorial to learn a new technique. If the overall commitment of making advanced blocks from month to month is just too much for you, ask the bee host if you could find a replacement to take your spot in the bee. But don't give up! Before joining your next bee, take a quick look at the skill levels of the other quilters involved, and see if you'd feel comfortable stepping in.

- **YOU ARE LOOKING FOR A MORE CHALLENGING BEE WITH A HIGHER COMMITMENT LEVEL** If the blocks are too simple for your taste, it's best to finish out the bee as a team player. For the next round, let the group know that you'd like to start another bee for swapping advanced blocks and see if anyone would like to join you.

Giving Back

It didn't take me long to realize that the online quilting community is filled with genuine, giving people. From charity quilting bees to quilters pitching in to welcome a new baby into the world, a bit of philanthropy always seems to come along with the act of quilting! As a participant in "quilting together," I've always found something meaningful in coming together to create.

Some bees exist solely to make blankets for those who are less fortunate. Other groups work together to make items for charity auctions or raffles. Cindy (whose work is featured on page 71) raised $6,400 for relief for developing countries by entering a handmade quilt in a charity auction and raising awareness and support through her blog.

As a quilter who loves fabric and thread, I can think of no better way to serve the world in need than to partner with organizations that support charity quilting. That is why the *String Circles* quilt (page 104) will be auctioned off and the proceeds donated to a special charity. For more information on how to bid on the quilt and to get involved in the charity quilting movement, visit this book's online home at modernbeebook.com.

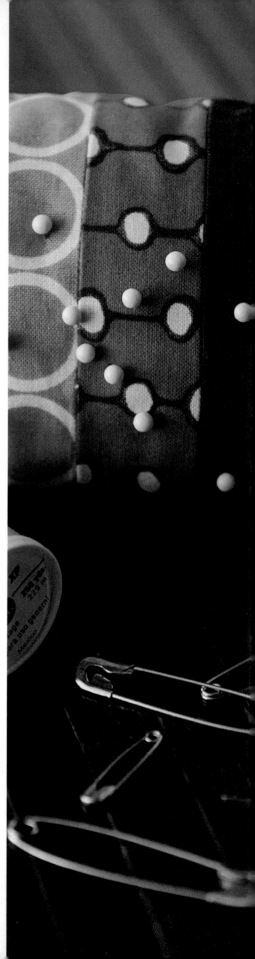

Being in an online sewing community has totally changed my life! I have more friends now than ever. There are people out there that honestly care about me, and we just communicate via email, blogs, and social media outlets. That means a lot to me, and I'm no longer a hermit quilter. —SUKIE NEWBOLD

I've made many close friends online. I have met several in real life, and it has just strengthened our friendship. I also like the fact that I've become friends with many women who are very different in age, but we share a common passion and age doesn't matter at all. —CINDY WIENS

Being part of a quilting bee gives me a chance to try on other styles and colors and pushes me outside my comfort zone on a small scale. It's only one block. I love the chance to sew with friends and make new ones. Thanks to bees and swaps, my home has many gorgeous handmade items from all over the world. —ADRIANNE OVE

I am so happy to be a part of the modern quilting community. I've made so many wonderful friends who have been amazing influences and support for me in my life. I am continually inspired by the amazing quilters I know strictly online as well as those I have met in real life. It's a lot like finding your tribe; I feel like I belong with the quilty people. —ELIZABETH DACKSON

Quilting and sewing has really been the first true hobby that I've had as an adult. I use it as my few minutes or hours of "me" time that I get to spend each day working and creating down in my sewing room. When I started my blog, I intended it as a way to chronicle my projects and never imagined finding a warm and welcoming online community of quilters. —JESSICA KELLY

A REAL COMMUNITY

What's special about the online sewing community?

Being part of the online sewing community has drastically changed my creative life. I feel like there are people out there who really "get" me and my craft, as opposed to other friends who do still appreciate what I do but don't quite understand it on the same level. I now have people with whom I can share my creative process, who can offer insights on my latest projects, and who actually understand when I hunt down that one print to complete a fabric collection—and then hoard said collection! —ELENA ROSCOE

The sewing and quilting community is so welcoming and friendly, both online and in person. I've made great friends, and it's wonderful to connect with people that share your passion. It's also been a great outlet for me as a stay-at-home mom. Sometimes being at home with young children can feel a bit isolating, and I've enjoyed connecting online with friends in similar situations. —JENNIFER MATHIS

My quilting friends are my first "grown-up" friends that I know I will have for life. I have been lucky to meet some of the most genuine, caring people through this hobby. I have new evidence every day that I mean something to others, that their influence is effecting a positive change in me, and that what we do together will influence others for good. —COLLEEN MOLEN

JANUARY | FEBRUARY

MARCH | APRIL

Beginner Blocks

PIECING SQUARES AND RECTANGLES

Ninety-degree angles are far from boring, as you'll learn from these striking, modern quilts. Build a colorful and fresh Log Cabin and even octagons from precut squares. In this section, we'll introduce you to patchwork shapes with right angles and four sides, the serene and familiar shapes that are ideal building blocks for strong, graphic quilt designs. Piecing simple squares is a great way to perfect your ¼″ seams while learning to follow a basic block pattern.

JANUARY
Mosaic Tiles

Made by Sukie Newbold • Fabric: assorted novelty prints

Remember the sliding tiles games where the goal is to move the tiles left or right to form a picture? The Mosaic Tiles block is a great place for quilting beginners to get started piecing squares and rectangles. Squares of novelty print fabrics are framed in a fabric border and then sliced into four quadrants. The eye tries to visually piece the images back together, but with a variety of mixed-up prints, the puzzle look makes this block stand out.

Block size: 11″ × 11″ unfinished, 10½″ × 10½″ finished

MATERIALS

- Black: 2¼ yards for blocks
- Prints: 57 assorted 5″ × 5″ squares for blocks
- Dark black: 1 yard for sashing
- Binding: ⅝ yard
- Backing: 4 yards
- Batting: 68″ × 68″

CUTTING INSTRUCTIONS

WOF = *width of fabric*

Black:

- Cut 24 strips 2″ × WOF. Give 2 strips to each bee member. Bee members will subcut the first strip into 6 rectangles 2″ × 5″ and 1 rectangle 2″ × 8″, and the second strip into 5 rectangles 2″ × 8″. The quilt requires 38 strips total.

Prints:

- Cut 3 assorted 5″ × 5″ squares for each bee member (36 squares total). The quilt requires 57 squares total.

Dark black:

- Cut 4 strips 8″ × WOF, joining pieces as needed for length. From the strips, cut the following:

    1 strip 8″ × 32″

    1 strip 8″ × 21½″

    1 strip 8″ × 60½″

Binding:

- Cut 7 strips 2½″ × WOF.

Block Assembly

1. With the right sides facing, stitch 2″ × 5″ rectangles to the top and bottom edges of a 5″ × 5″ print square. Press the seams open.

2. Stitch 2″ × 8″ rectangles to the sides of the unit. Press the seams open.

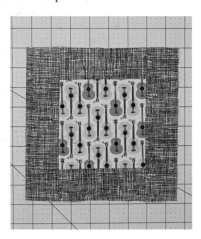

3. Cut the 8″ × 8″ framed square into quadrants.

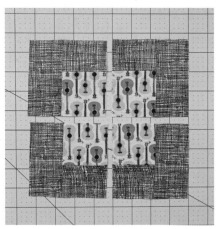

4. Repeat Steps 1–3 with the other 5″ × 5″ print squares.

5. Mix up the quadrants at random and select 9 to make the block. Arrange them as shown, noting the placement of the featured print: *Row 1 (bottom right, top right, bottom right), Row 2 (bottom left, top left, bottom left), and Row 3 (same as Row 1).*

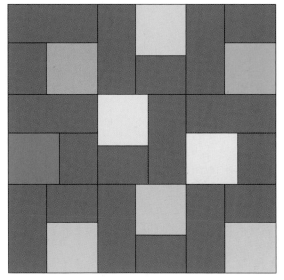

6. Arrange and sew 3 rows of 3 units each. Join the rows. Extra units should be mailed back to the host for making additional blocks.

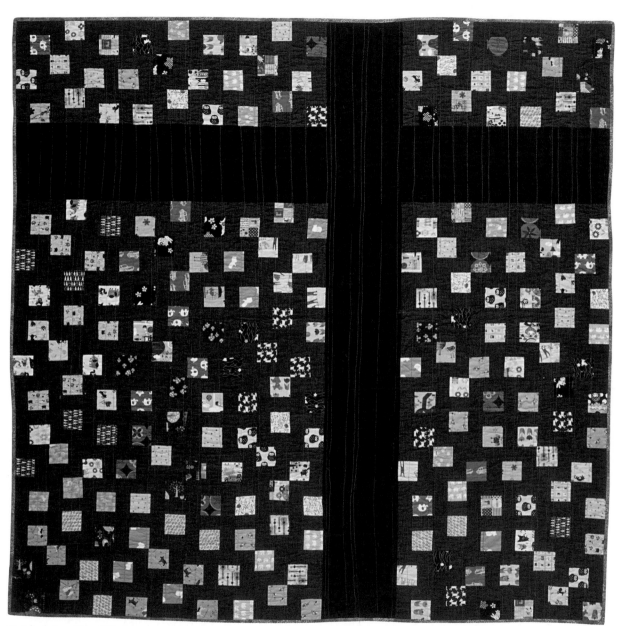

Finished size: 60″ × 60″

Quilt Construction

Refer to the quilt photo (page 35) and to the quilt assembly diagram (below).

1. Arrange 25 blocks into 5 rows of 5 blocks each.

2. In the first row, join the first 3 blocks and stitch them to a long side of the 8″ × 32″ background strip. Press.

3. Join the last 2 blocks in the first row and stitch them to a long side of the 8″ × 21½″ background strip. Press.

4. Join the first 3 blocks in each of the remaining rows. Join the rows and sew them to the section from Step 2. Press.

5. Join the last 2 blocks in each of the remaining rows. Join the rows and sew them to the section from Step 3. Press.

6. Sew the completed sections to the 8″ × 60½″ background strip. Press.

7. Layer, quilt, and bind the quilt (pages 116–121).

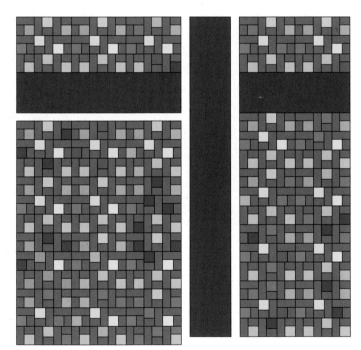

Quilt assembly diagram

Seam Allowances

In hand quilting and piecing, ¼″ seam allowances are recommended. When piecing by machine, the standard seam allowance needs to be a hair smaller because the double threads of a sewing machine take up room. For this reason, a scant ¼″ seam is recommended for all patchwork done on a sewing machine.

To get a scant ¼″ seam, use a quarter-inch patchwork foot and line up the edge of the fabric with the rightmost edge of the foot. If you do not have a quarter-inch foot, use a general-purpose foot and adjust the needle until the distance from the needle to the rightmost edge of the presser foot is just shy of ¼″.

The seam allowance will affect the size of the finished quilt blocks, so it's especially important when sewing with bee members who have different machines and settings. A scant ¼″ seam is recommended for all the blocks in this book.

Chain Piecing

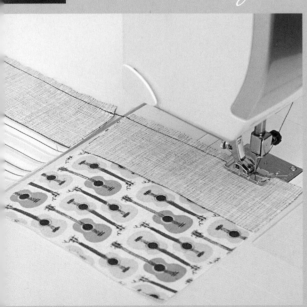

When piecing multiple sets of identical blocks, chain piecing the blocks saves time and uses less thread. To chain piece the mosaic tile blocks, sew the top strip on all three squares. Do not cut the thread until all three squares have made it through this step. Simply pick up the fabric and lift it out of the way with the thread still connected.

When those three squares are sewn, clip the threads and attach the next set of strips to each block. Repeat this method to finish the sides.

Playing Cards

Made by Jennifer Mathis • Fabric: Washi by Rashida Coleman-Hale, Timeless Treasures

This pint-sized quilt makes a great baby play mat or accent piece. Piece together squares and rectangles to make waves of modern playing cards. You can assign bee members specific prints in three color groups for a coordinated set of finished quilt blocks, or let them choose the placement for a more random finished look. Jennifer's hand stitching secures the quilt and adds a soft, handmade finish to the modern prints and graphic shapes.

Block size: 15½″ × 13″ unfinished, 15″ × 12½″ finished

MATERIALS

- **Tan:** 2¼ yards for blocks and sashing
- **Prints:** ¼ yard each of 9 prints
- **Binding:** ½ yard
- **Backing:** 3 yards (pieced crosswise)
- **Batting:** 53″ × 66″

CUTTING INSTRUCTIONS

WOF = width of fabric

Tan:

- Cut 6 strips 5½″ × WOF. From each strip, subcut 2 pieces each (12 total) of A–E below and give each bee member 1 piece each:

    A: 3½″ × 5½″ (12 total)

    B: 4″ × 5½″ (12 total)

    C: 1½″ × 5½″ (12 total)

    D: 6″ × 5½″ (12 total)

    E: 5½″ × 5½″ (12 total)

- From remaining yardage, cut 1 lengthwise-grain sashing strip 8″ × 45½″. From scraps, cut 12 F pieces, and give each bee member 1 piece each:

    F: 2″ × 5½″ (12 total)

Prints:

- For each bee member, cut 3 sets of the following 3 pieces (a1, a2, and b) in different prints:

  a1: 5½″ × 3½″ (36 total)

  a2: 3½″ × 3″ (36 total)

  b: 3½″ × 3″ (36 total)

- From ¼-yard pieces of print fabric (9 prints):

  Cut 1 strip 5½″ × WOF from each print. *Unfold* and subcut 4 pieces 3½″ × 5½″ (a1). Trim the remaining 5½″ strips to 3½″ and subcut 8 pieces 3½″ × 3″ (4 each of a2 and b).

Binding:

- Cut 6 strips 2½″ × WOF.

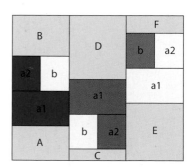

Block Assembly

1. Each unit within the block has 3 pieces: a1, a2, and b. Sew a2 and b together along the 3½″ sides. Press the seams open.

2. Refer to the block diagram for the placement of contrasting piece b. Sew a2/b to a1 along the 5½″ edges. Repeat for the other 2 units.

3. Arrange the tan pieces and units in order according to the diagram. Stitch together using a scant ¼″ seam allowance.

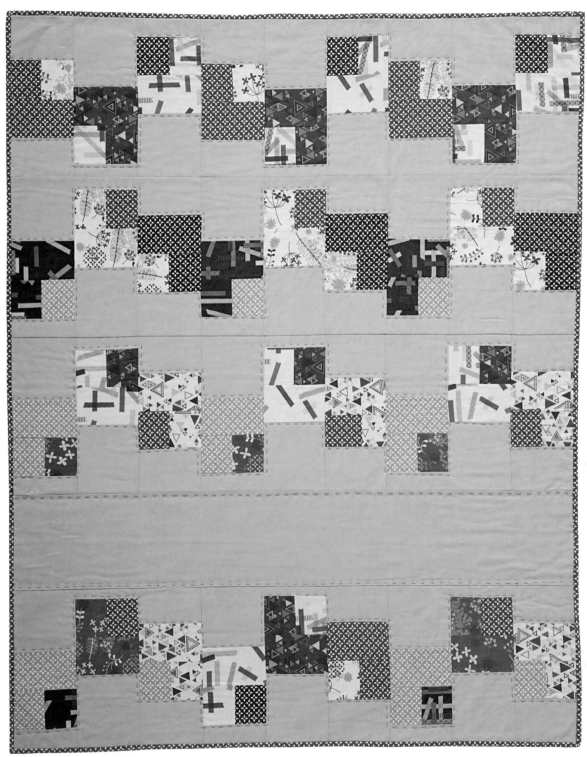

Finished size: 45″ × 57½″

Pressing Seams

While some quilters prefer the quick and easy method of pressing seams to one side, I prefer to press seams open whenever possible. Many quilters agree that this gives patchwork a precise and crisp look.

It's easy to finger-press pieced seams open using your fingernail or a wooden seam-pressing tool. After joining two squares of fabric, place the fabric right side down on a table. Starting at the base of the seam, use the edge of your fingernail to separate the fabric along the seam. With the back of your nail, press the seam open. You can later reinforce the seam with an iron by pressing down and lifting up on the open seams. When pressing, do not overheat the iron or swipe from side to side, which can distort the fabric.

In some cases, such as in the center of a patchwork star, pressing the seams open creates too much bulk. In this case, press seams toward the darker fabric. Try both methods, pressing seams open and pressing to one side, to see which one you prefer.

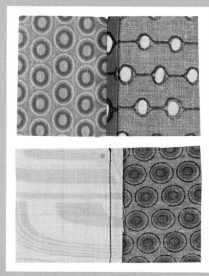

Seams pressed open (top); seams pressed to one side (bottom)

Quilt Construction

Refer to the quilt photo (page 41) and to the quilt assembly diagram (below).

1. Arrange 12 blocks into 4 rows of 3 blocks each.

2. Sew the blocks into rows. Press.

3. Join the first 3 rows. Sew the joined rows and the bottom row to the 8″ × 45½″ sashing strip. Press.

4. Layer, quilt, and bind the quilt (pages 116–121).

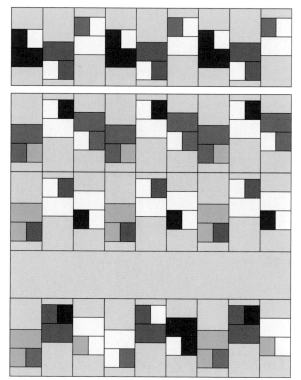

Quilt assembly diagram

Bluebell's Cabin

Made by Adrianne Ove • Fabric: Half Moon Modern by MoMo, Moda

A versatile and classic design, the Log Cabin is a block built from the center out, with countless variations based on the fabric used and its placement. Adrianne's version is freshened up with a white background alternating with bright, graphic prints. The same block design could be completed in all solids, monochromatic prints, or a scrappy rainbow of prints for a totally different look.

Block size: 12½″ × 12½″ unfinished, 12″ × 12″ finished

MATERIALS

- **Prints:** 14 fat quarters or 48 strips 2½″ × WOF for blocks. For greater variety, use 18 fat quarters or 60 strips 2½″ × WOF.

- **White:** 3 yards for blocks, sashing, and borders

- **Binding:** ¾ yard

- **Backing:** 5 yards

- **Batting:** 66″ × 94″

CUTTING INSTRUCTIONS

WOF = width of fabric

Prints:

- From each fat quarter, cut 7 strips 2½″ × 20″–22″ or subcut 2½″ strips into 2½″ × 20″–22″ pieces for a total of 96–126 strips. Give each bee member 1 strip each of 8 to 10 different prints.

White:

- For each bee member, cut 2 block centers 2½″ × 2½″ (24 total).

- For each bee member, cut 2 strips 1½″ × WOF (24 total).

- For sashing and borders, cut 20 strips 2½″ × WOF, joining as needed to piece longer strips. From these strips, cut the following:

  18 strips 2½″ × 12½″ for sashing between the blocks

  5 strips 2½″ × 54½″ for sashing between the rows

  2 strips 2½″ × 82½″ for side borders

  2 strips 2½″ × 58½″ for top and bottom borders

Binding:

- Cut 8 strips 2½″ × WOF.

Block Assembly

1. From the 1½″ white strips and 2½″ print fabric strips, cut 1 piece of each as indicated. The numbers correspond with the block pattern below.

CENTER: White	1.	2½″ × 2½″
	2.	2½″ × 2½″
FIRST RING: Prints	3.	2½″ × 4½″
	4.	2½″ × 4½″
	5.	2½″ × 6½″
	6.	1½″ × 6½″
SECOND RING: White	7.	1½″ × 7½″
	8.	1½″ × 7½″
	9.	1½″ × 8½″
	10.	2½″ × 8½″
THIRD RING: Prints	11.	2½″ × 10½″
	12.	2½″ × 10½″
	13.	2½″ × 12½″

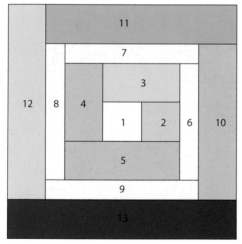

Sew pieces in numerical order.

2. Stitch center piece 1 to piece 2 using a scant ¼″ seam allowance. Press seams open.

3. Stitch piece 3 to the block. Press seams open.

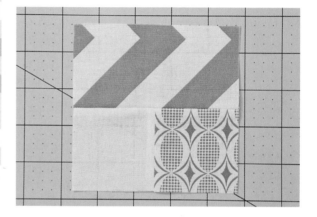

4. Continue to rotate the block and attach pieces in order as indicated in the diagram. Make 24 blocks.

Quilt Construction

Refer to the quilt photo and the quilt assembly diagram (below).

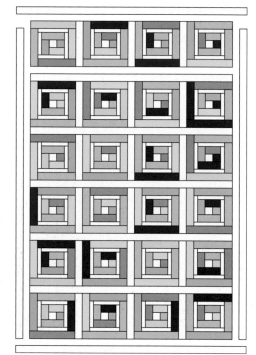

Quilt assembly diagram

1. Arrange 24 blocks into 6 rows of 4 blocks each. Sew the 2½″ × 12½″ sashing pieces between the blocks in each row. Press.

2. Sew the rows of blocks to the 2½″ × 54½″ sashing pieces. Press.

3. Add the side borders. Press.

4. Add the top and bottom borders. Press.

5. Layer, quilt, and bind the quilt (pages 116–121).

Finished size: 58″ × 86″

Cutting Tools and Fabric Grain

A quilter's fabric-cutting essentials include a rotary cutter, clear ruler, and self-healing cutting mat. These each come in a variety of sizes, but I most often use a 45mm rotary cutter, a 6″ × 24″ ruler, and an 18″ × 24″ cutting mat. You may also wish to invest in a 12½″ square ruler for accurately trimmed blocks such as those in *String Circles* (page 104). A smaller ruler such as 6½″ × 6½″ is handy for trimming small pieces. A good pair of fabric scissors is also a great investment for quilters.

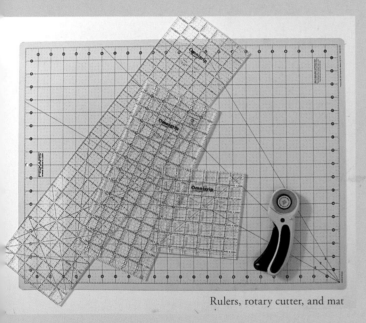

Rulers, rotary cutter, and mat

Before cutting fabric into strips, use a rotary cutter and ruler to trim off both selvages (the rough edges where the fabric name is often printed) for a clean edge. This is called *squaring up* the fabric.

When examined closely, it's easy to see that quilting fabric has a distinct grid of threads running lengthwise and widthwise, known as the *grain*.

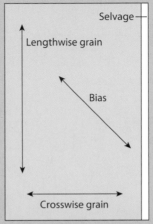

WIDTH OF FABRIC (CROSSWISE GRAIN)
When cutting fabric for quilt blocks, cut along the crosswise grain. You can also think of this as cutting from selvage to selvage, or across the width of the fabric. Fabric requirements in this book are based on a 42″ fabric width after the selvages are removed.

LENGTH OF FABRIC (LENGTHWISE GRAIN)
The lengthwise grain of the fabric runs along the length of the fabric. For instance, 1 yard of fabric is 36″ in length. If you can no longer tell which is the length or width of the fabric, take a section in your hands and pull in both directions. The lengthwise grain will have less stretch to it than the crosswise grain.

BIAS   Fabric cut along the bias is cut diagonally across the lengthwise and crosswise grains. This fabric is most often used for bias bindings (page 118) and in other cases where very stretchy fabric is preferable, like the binding of a curved place mat.

Painter's Palette

Made by Megan Bohr • Fabric: Kona solids, Robert Kaufman

Would you believe that this colorful circle of octagons is actually made by sewing together four-sided shapes—basic squares, rectangles, and strips? These snowball blocks are easy to make in assembly-line fashion. The arrangement even plays up symmetry and the flow of the color wheel!

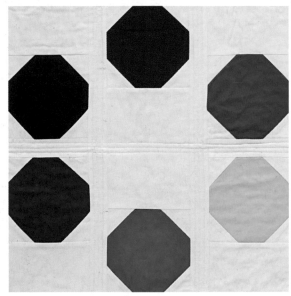

Block size: 16″ × 16″ unfinished, 15½″ × 15½″ finished

MATERIALS

- **Solids:** 1 fat quarter (18″ × 22″) each of 6 different colors for blocks
- **White:** 4 yards (2⅞ yards for blocks, 1⅛ yards for sashing and borders)
- **Binding:** ⅝ yard
- **Backing:** 3½ yards (pieced crosswise)
- **Batting:** 63″ × 80″

CUTTING INSTRUCTIONS

WOF = width of fabric

Solids:

- Cut each fat quarter into 5″ strips. Subcut into 5″ × 5″ squares, for 12 squares per color (72 total). Give each bee member 1 square in each of the 6 colors.

White:

- For each bee member, cut the individual pieces needed for each block:

  1 rectangle 5″ × 7″ (12 total)

  2 rectangles 1½″ × 5″ (24 total)

  4 rectangles 3¼″ × 5″ (48 total)

  2 rectangles 1½″ × 16″ (24 total)

  24 squares 2″ × 2″ (288 total)

- For sashing and borders, cut 14 strips 2½″ × WOF, joining as needed for length. From these strips, cut the following:

  9 strips 2½″ × 16″ for sashing between blocks

  4 strips 2½″ × 68½″ for sashing between rows and for side borders

  2 strips 2½″ × 55″ for top and bottom borders

Binding:

- Cut 7 strips 2½″ × WOF.

Block Assembly

1. Place 4 white squares 2″ × 2″ on top of the corners of a solid square 5″ × 5″. Use a ruler and pencil or Hera marker to mark a diagonal line from corner to corner on the white squares as shown.

Mark squares diagonally.

TIP: A Hera marker, also called a tracing spatula, is a plastic or wooden tool with a curved edge that can be used to crease lines in fabric. I also use Alex Anderson's 4-in-1 Essential Sewing Tool (by C&T Publishing) to make the creases (Resources, page 127).

2. Sew on the lines. (Contrasting thread is used in the photo below just as an example.) Trim the seam allowance to ¼″.

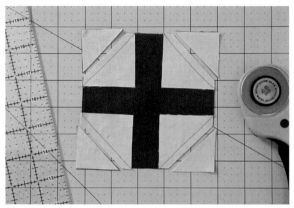

Stitch and trim corners.

3. Press seams outward toward the white. Repeat with the remaining white and solid squares to make a unit of each color.

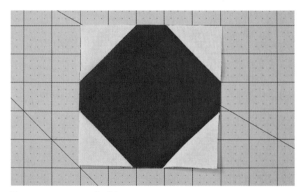

Press seams toward white.

4. Sew a rectangle 3¼" × 5" to an edge of the purple, blue, orange, and yellow units. Join the purple and blue units with a 1½" × 5" white rectangle. Repeat to join the orange and yellow units. Sew the 5" × 7" white rectangle between the red and green units to make the block's center column. Sew the columns to the white rectangles 1½" × 16".

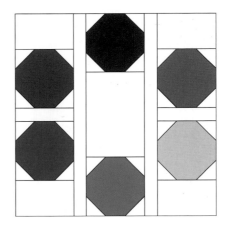

Quilt Construction

Refer to the quilt photo (page 52) and to the quilt assembly diagram (at right).

1. Arrange the blocks in 3 columns of 4 blocks each. Sew the 2½" × 16" sashing pieces between the blocks in each column. Press.

2. Sew the columns to the 2½" × 68½" sashing pieces. Press.

3. Add the side borders. Press.

4. Add the top and bottom borders. Press.

5. Layer, quilt, and bind the quilt (pages 116–121).

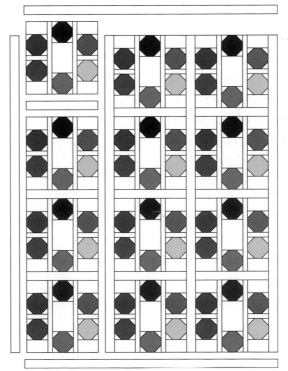

Quilt assembly diagram

Finished size: 54½″ × 72″

Fabric Colors

Megan's block provides a good illustration of the color wheel, a helpful tool for choosing fabrics that will work well together. There are no set rules to choosing colors for a quilt, but understanding the way colors interact with each other is a great place to start!

WARM OR COOL? In general, reds, oranges, and yellows are *warm colors*. Blues, greens, and purples are *cool colors*. There is some overlap, however. If a purple has more of a reddish hint to it, the fabric could be considered warm, for instance. In general, warm colors are vivid and tend to "jump off the page," while cool colors are calm and soothing and tend to recede.

PRIMARY, SECONDARY, TERTIARY Red, yellow and blue are considered *primary colors*, and they form a triangle in Megan's block. Orange, green, and purple are considered *secondary colors* and are each located between a pair of primary colors. *Tertiary colors* (not pictured) are a mixture of primary and secondary colors, such as yellow-green and red-orange.

ANALOGOUS COLORS such as yellow, yellow-green, and green are next to each other on the color wheel. Using an analogous color scheme has a harmonious and serene effect.

NEUTRAL COLORS such as black, white, and gray can be interspersed with choices from the color wheel to change the intensity of the colors. For instance, adding white fabric to a quilt will give it a brighter tint, while adding gray fabric will give the surrounding colors in the quilt a dustier tone.

COMPLEMENTARY COLORS such as orange and blue are opposite each other on the color wheel, and the high-contrast pairing tends to make a design look vibrant or pop.

When choosing colors for a quilt, it's important to go with your instinct and choose colors you like together, rather than sticking to hard-and-fast rules. However, it often helps to know these basics so you aren't surprised when a finished quilt has a certain look or feel.

ANALOGOUS

NEUTRAL

COMPLEMENTARY

MAY | JUNE

JULY | AUGUST

Confident Beginner Blocks

INCORPORATING TRIANGLES

Visually, triangles are considered to be energetic shapes, meaning they can direct movement based on which way they point. But why is it that three-sided shapes incite fear in many quilters? Commonly seen in traditional quilt patterns, triangles offer a great skill builder for quilters looking to piece with precision. In this section, you'll learn to sew half-square triangles two ways, pair triangles with squares and rectangles, and make Flying Geese units to create four unique quilts.

Come Together

Made by Elizabeth Dackson • Fabric: Echo by Lotta Jansdotter, Windham Fabrics

This block marries the familiarity of sewing squares and strips with the new (to some of us) skill of making quilts with triangles. When the blocks are joined to make the quilt top, the gray corner triangles come together to form perfect diamond centers. The centers of the blocks are customized with different color combinations, using fabric from the same collection. This quilt would also look great with scrappy prints or all solids—use your creativity to personalize this bold, yet uniform, design.

Block size: 20½" × 20½" unfinished, 20" × 20" finished

MATERIALS

- **White:** 2¼ yards for blocks
- **Prints:** 2¼ yards total of assorted prints for blocks
- **Teal solid:** ⅞ yard for blocks
- **Gray print:** ⅝ yard for blocks
- **Binding:** ⅝ yard
- **Backing:** 5 yards
- **Batting:** 68" × 88"

CUTTING INSTRUCTIONS

WOF = width of fabric

White:

- For each bee member, cut 8 squares 4½" × 4½" (96 total) and 1 square 7" × 7" (12 total).

Prints:

- For each bee member, cut 1 square 4½" × 4½" for center print (12 total).

- For each bee member, cut 2 strips 2½" × WOF (24 total). Give each bee member 1 strip in each of 2 coordinating prints.

Teal:

- For each bee member, cut 4 squares 4½" × 4½" (48 total).

Gray:

- For each bee member, cut 1 square 7" × 7" (12 total).

Binding:

- Cut 8 strips 2½" × WOF.

Block Assembly

1. Cut and stitch 2 print rectangles 2½″ × 4½″ to the top and bottom of the 4½″ × 4½″ center square. Press the seams open.

2. Cut and stitch 2 rectangles 2½″ × 8½″ of the same print to the sides of the unit.

3. Using the second print, cut and stitch 2 rectangles 2½″ × 8½″ to the top and bottom of the unit and 2 rectangles 2½″ × 12½″ to the sides of the unit.

4. To make half-square triangle units, place a white square 7″ × 7″ and a gray square 7″ × 7″ right sides together. Sew a scant ¼″ seam around the perimeter, joining the squares.

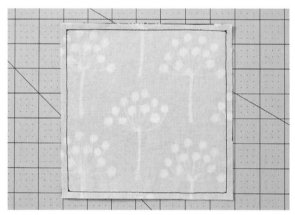

Stitch edges of squares.

5. Using a rotary cutter, cut twice diagonally to make 4 half-square triangle units.

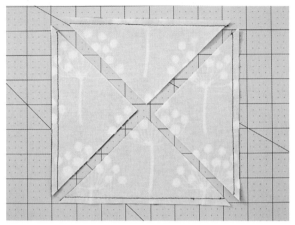

Cut twice diagonally.

6. Press the seams open. Trim each half-square triangle unit to 4½″ × 4½″ using a clear ruler with a 45° mark to line up with the diagonal seam.

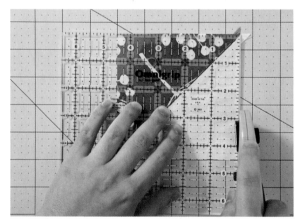

Trim half-square triangle unit.

7. Sew a white square to opposite sides of the 4 teal squares to make 4 pieced units. Sew 2 units to the top and bottom of the framed center square.

8. Sew a half-square triangle unit to the ends of the remaining white and teal units. Sew to the sides of the center square, so the gray corner triangles point outward.

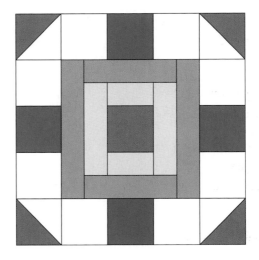

Quilt Construction

Refer to the quilt photo (page 60) and to the quilt assembly diagram (at right).

1. Arrange 12 blocks into 4 rows of 3 blocks each.

2. Sew the blocks into rows. Press.

3. Join the rows. Press.

4. Layer, quilt, and bind the quilt (pages 116–121).

Quilt assembly diagram

Finished size: 60″ × 80″

Block Sizes: Finished or Unfinished?

When sewing with a bee, make sure to clarify the final size of your block in one of two ways. An *unfinished block* size refers to the blocks you receive back from bee mates. A *finished block* size refers to the size of the block as it appears in the quilt. For Elizabeth's quilt, the unfinished block size is 20½″, but the blocks will lose ¼″ on each side when they are joined with neighboring blocks. This makes the finished block size 20″.

If you say a *finished block* should be a certain size, the bee members should know not to trim too much off the block by accident. To be on the safe side, always specify whether you expect bee members to trim their blocks to a certain size or you'd prefer to do the final trimming yourself.

JUNE
Stacked Windmills

Made by Jeni Baker • Fabric: It's a Hoot by MoMo, Moda; Heath by Alexander Henry

Jeni's Stacked Windmills block is perfect for showing off coordinating prints from a fat quarter bundle. When arranged in color groups, the half-square triangles form the arms and central spoke of the windmill, for a modern block accentuated by simple sashing and cornerstones. Bee members can personalize their blocks by choosing the placement of each print.

Block size: 15½" × 15½" unfinished, 15" × 15" finished

MATERIALS

- **Prints:** ¼ yard each of 24 different prints for blocks

- **White:** 3½ yards for blocks, sashing, and borders

- **Binding:** ⅝ yard

- **Backing:** 3½ yards (pieced crosswise)

- **Batting:** 63" × 80"

CUTTING INSTRUCTIONS

WOF = width of fabric

Prints:

- For each bee member, cut 1 strip 5" × 15" of 4 different prints (48 total). Bee members will subcut each strip into 5" × 5" squares (and will have several squares left over).

- From print fabric scraps, cut 6 squares 3" × 3" for cornerstones.

White:

- Cut 14 strips 5" × WOF. Subcut into squares 5" × 5" and give each bee member 9 squares (108 total).

- For sashing and borders, cut 16 strips 3" × WOF, joining as needed for length. From these strips, cut the following:

  17 pieces 3" × 15½" for sashing between the blocks

  2 strips 3" × 50½" for top and bottom borders

  2 strips 3" × 73" for side borders

Binding:

- Cut 7 strips 2½" × WOF.

Block Assembly

1. For the half-square triangle units, use 9 white squares 5″ × 5″. Use 3 squares each from 2 prints (6 total), 2 squares from another print (2 total), and a square from the final print.

2. Place a white square 5″ × 5″ and a print square 5″ × 5″ right sides together. Sew a scant ¼″ seam around the perimeter, joining the squares.

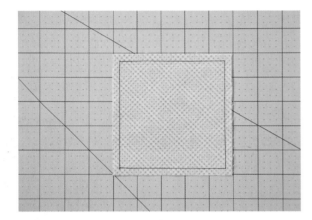

3. Using a rotary cutter, cut twice diagonally, making 4 half-square triangle units.

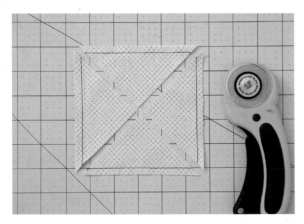

4. Press the seams open. Trim each half-square triangle unit to 3″ × 3″, using a clear ruler with a 45° angle to line with up the diagonal seam.

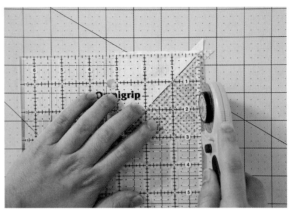

5. Make 36 half-square triangle units and arrange according to the block diagram, which has 6 rows of 6 units each.

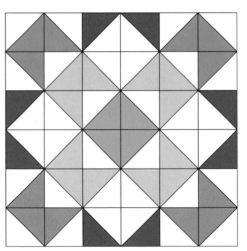

Quilt Construction

Refer to the quilt photo and quilt assembly diagram (below).

1. Arrange 12 blocks into 4 rows of 3 blocks each. Sew the 3″ × 15½″ sashing pieces between the blocks in each row. Press.

2. Arrange the remaining 3″ × 15½″ sashing pieces and cornerstone squares 3″ × 3″ between the rows. Join the sashing and cornerstones. Press.

3. Join the block rows and the sashing and cornerstone rows. Press.

4. Add the top and bottom borders. Press.

5. Add the side borders. Press.

6. Layer, quilt, and bind the quilt (pages 116–121).

Quilt assembly diagram

Finished size: 55″ × 72½″

Pinning and Ripping

Two essentials tools for piecing quilt blocks are a good seam ripper and plenty of sewing pins. Both are available in many varieties, but I prefer to use a seam ripper with a thick handle for comfort. I also like to use long pins with brightly colored pinheads so I can see them clearly when sewing.

When piecing the rows and columns of a block such as Stacked Windmill, symmetry and alignment of the seams are important to the block design. To join two rows, place a pin near each of the seams.

While sewing, use your free hand and another pin to gently tug the fabric so the seams stay properly aligned while under the sewing machine's presser foot.

If the seams do not align as planned, use a seam ripper to gently pull out the threads where seams do not match. Repin and stitch again so that the seams align. This is a great block to practice aligning seams.

Cordelia's Garden

Made by Katie Bowlby • Fabric: Kona solids, Robert Kaufman

12 Bee Members • 1 block each

Vintage quilts can serve as priceless family heirlooms, providing comfort and warmth from one generation to the next. Katie was inspired to quilt a modern version of her great-great-grandmother Cordelia's handwork. By adapting the design, she made this quilt easier to piece with no Y-seams. The bold, contrasting blocks bring a modern twist to a well-loved tradition.

Block size: 12½″ × 12½″ unfinished, 12″ × 12″ finished

MATERIALS

- **Gray:** 3¼ yards for blocks, sashing, and borders

- **Purple:** 1½ yards for blocks

- **Blue:** 1 yard for blocks

- **Green:** ¾ yard for blocks

- **Binding:** ⅝ yard

- **Backing:** 3¾ yards (pieced crosswise)

- **Batting:** 66″ × 78″

CUTTING INSTRUCTIONS

WOF = width of fabric

Gray:

- For each bee member, cut 16 squares 2½″ × 2½″ (192 total) and 4 squares 3½″ × 3½″ (48 total).

- For each contrasting block, cut 12 squares 2½″ × 2½″ (48 total) and 4 squares 3½″ × 3½″ (16 total).

Gray, continued:

- For sashing and borders, cut 17 strips 2½″ × WOF, joining as needed to piece longer strips. From these strips, cut the following:

    12 pieces 2½″ × 12½″ for sashing between blocks

    5 strips 2½″ × 54½″ for sashing between rows and for side borders

    4 strips 2½″ × 58½″ for top and bottom borders

Purple:

- For each bee member, cut 4 squares 2½″ × 2½″ (48 total) and 4 squares 3½″ × 3½″ (48 total).

- For each contrasting block, cut 12 squares 2½″ × 2½″ (48 total) and 4 squares 3½″ × 3½″ (16 total).

- For bottom border, cut 2 strips 4½″ × WOF. Join and trim to 4½″ × 58½″.

Blue:

- For each bee member, cut 4 squares 3½″ × 3½″ (48 total).

- For each of 3 contrasting blocks, cut 4 squares 2½″ × 2½″ (12 total).

- For top border, cut 2 strips 4½″ × WOF. Join and trim to 4½″ × 58½″.

Green:

- For each bee member, cut 4 squares 3½″ × 3½″ (48 total).

- For 1 contrasting block, cut 4 squares 2½″ × 2½″.

Binding:

- Cut 7 strips 2½″ × WOF.

Block Assembly

1. To make the half-square triangles, place a gray square 3½″ × 3½″ on top of a colored square 3½″ × 3½″ with right sides together. With a ruler and pencil or Hera marker, mark a diagonal line across the top square.

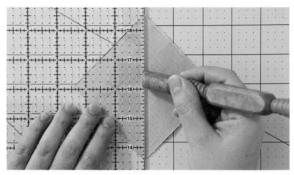

Mark square diagonally.

2. Sew ¼″ from the marked line on both sides.

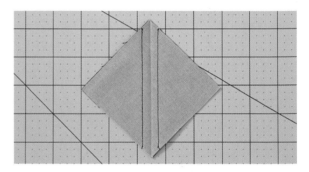

3. Cut on the marked line.

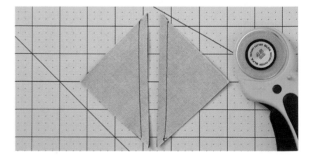

4. Press the seams open. Trim each half-square triangle to 2½″ × 2½″, using a clear ruler with a 45° mark to line up with the diagonal seam.

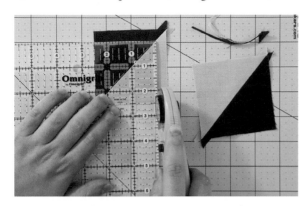

5. Repeat with the other gray and colored squares 3½″ × 3½″. To make all the half-square triangles needed for a block, repeat Steps 1–4 with the following combinations:

    2 purple and 2 blue squares

    2 purple and 2 green squares

    2 gray and 2 blue squares

    2 gray and 2 green squares

6. Arrange the units into the block. Sew into rows. Join the rows. Press.

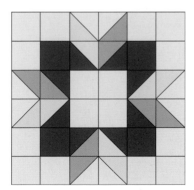

Contrasting Block

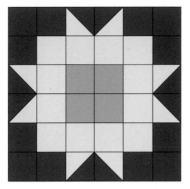

1. Make half-square triangles (Steps 1–4 in Block Assembly) using 4 gray and 4 purple squares 3½″ × 3½″. Trim the half-square triangle units to 2½″ × 2½″.

2. Arrange the remaining squares and half-square triangle units into the block. Sew into rows. Join the rows. Press.

Finished size: 58″ × 70″

Piecing Blocks

When joining a half-square triangle to a square of the same size, one unit is pieced (the triangle) and one unit is a single piece. If you have the choice, stack a pieced unit on top when feeding the unit through the sewing machine. This way, the seam is visible and it's less likely to bunch up while being fed through the machine.

When joining the rows within a block, you will likely have seams on both the top and the bottom layers. Take your time to pin the units carefully at all seams. Then stitch slowly, checking to ensure that seams stay flat and do not bunch as they go through the machine.

It's sometimes helpful to keep a sketch of the block nearby. Keep the block orientation in mind while joining the rows. Refer to the sketch before adding each new unit, making sure units are turned in the right direction. Pin together the units in each row, and then press the seams and lay out the rows in order. Refer to the diagram at each stage to avoid having to rip out seams because of inaccurate placement.

Quilt Construction

Refer to the quilt photo (page 69) and to the quilt assembly diagram (below).

1. Arrange 16 blocks into 4 rows of 4 blocks each. Arrange the contrasting blocks as shown in the diagram.

2. Sew the 2½″ × 12½″ sashing pieces between the blocks in each row. Press.

3. Sew the rows of blocks to the 2½″ × 54½″ sashing pieces to complete the quilt center. Press.

4. Add the side borders. Press.

5. Sew the top border pieces together. Press. Add to the quilt. Repeat with the bottom border pieces.

6. Layer, quilt, and bind the quilt (pages 116–121).

Quilt assembly diagram

Neon Ninja Star

Made by Cindy Wiens and quilted by Dea Oskerson • Fabric: Kona solids, Robert Kaufman; faux seersucker by Loralie Harris, Loralie Designs

The triangular Flying Geese block is a component of many modern and traditional quilt patterns. Upholstery fabric on the booths at a fast-food chain inspired Cindy's block design, which looks like a traditional Friendship Star block or a real-life ninja star. The vibrant colors and solitary black-and-white print offer strong visual contrast, but you can customize the quilt with a variety of prints or a softer palette of solids.

Block size: 12½″ × 12½″ unfinished, 12″ × 12″ finished

MATERIALS

- **Solids:** 1 fat quarter each of 10–14 different colors or 2¼ yards total of assorted colors for blocks

- **White:** 2¾ yards for blocks, sashing, and borders

- **Black stripe:** ⅓ yard for blocks

- **Binding:** ⅝ yard

- **Backing:** 3¼ yards (pieced crosswise)

- **Batting:** 58″ × 72″

CUTTING INSTRUCTIONS

WOF = width of fabric

Solids:

- Cut each fat quarter into 2 strips 3½″ × 22″ and 2 strips 2¾″ × 22″.

  Subcut strips into 3½″ × 3½″ squares (120–168 total) and 2¾″ × 6½″ rectangles (60–84 total). Give each bee member 8 squares and 4 rectangles in assorted colors. (You will have some left over.)

- For pieced border, cut a total of 14 rectangles 2¾″ × 12½″.

White:

- For each bee member, cut 1 strip 3½″ × WOF (12 total). Subcut into 4 rectangles 3½″ × 6½″ (48 total).

- For sashing and borders, cut the following:

  16 pieces 2¾″ × 12½″ for sashing between blocks

  5 lengthwise strips 2¾″ × 50″ for sashing between rows and top and bottom borders

  4 squares 2¾″ × 2¾″ for pieced border

  4 rectangles 2¾″ × 5″ for pieced border

Black stripe:

- For each bee member, cut 4 rectangles 1¼″ × 6½″ (48 total).

Binding:

- Cut 7 strips 2½″ × WOF.

Block Assembly

1. This block is constructed of 4 Flying Geese units. Each unit requires a white rectangle 2¾″ × 6½″ and 2 solid squares 3½″ × 3½″ (each a different color).

2. With a ruler and pencil or Hera marker, make a diagonal line from corner to corner on each of the solid squares. Place a solid square on the corner of the white rectangle. Sew on the line.

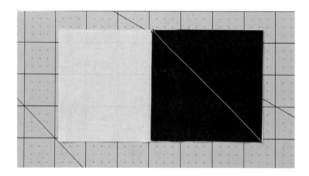

3. Trim the seam allowance to ¼″.

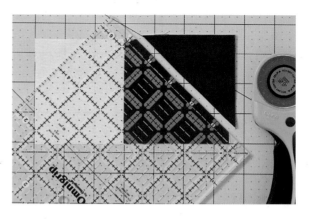

4. Press the seam open and turn right side up.

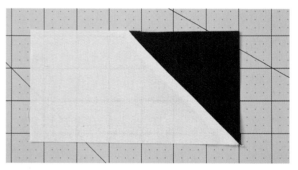

5. Place the other marked solid square on the other end of the rectangle with the diagonal line mirroring the first.

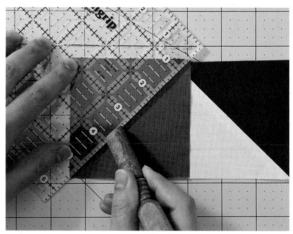

6. Sew on the line. Trim the seam allowance to ¼" and press the seam open.

7. Repeat to make 4 Flying Geese units. Use the colors randomly.

8. Stitch a solid 2¾" × 6½" rectangle to the base of each Flying Geese unit.

9. Stitch a black striped rectangle to the long edge of each solid rectangle from the previous step.

10. Arrange the blocks so that none of the same colors touch each other. Join together the 4 units as shown in the diagram, making sure all triangles face the correct way, with points facing clockwise.

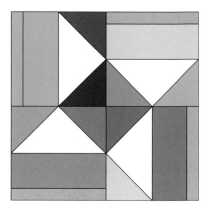

Finished size: 49½" × 63¾"

Prewashing Fabrics

I have a confession: I seldom prewash my fabric before making a quilt. Other quilters consistently prewash their fabrics. So what's a quilter to do? It's probably a good idea to try both methods to see whether you prefer to prewash, dry, and press your fabric or just dive right in.

I try to buy high-quality fabric that's not likely to bleed in the wash. If you purchase high-quality fabrics from a quilt shop rather than from a discount store, there is a lesser chance that the colors will bleed at all. However, some quilters find that dark blue, purple, and red fabrics have a tendency to bleed in the laundry. When working with bright fabrics in concentrated colors, such as those in *Neon Ninja Star*, it's often a good idea to prewash fabrics to prevent colors from bleeding onto the white.

To prewash fabrics, toss them in the washing machine with similar colors. Wash brights with cold water and your normal detergent. Warm water can be used for midrange colors and hot water for whites. If you are worried about bleeding, try color-absorbing sheets, sold with other laundry-care products. They look like dryer sheets but help absorb fabric dyes in the wash. If the fabric bleeds after you have finished a quilt, the liquid product Synthrapol can be added to the laundry with hot water to help absorb dyes in a stained quilt or garment.

Quilt Construction

Refer to the quilt photo (previous page) and to the quilt assembly diagram (below).

1. Arrange 12 blocks into 4 rows of 3 blocks each. Sew the 2¾" × 12½" sashing pieces between the blocks and at the ends of each row.

2. Add solid rectangles 2¾" × 12½" to the ends of each row.

3. Sew the 2¾" × 49½" sashing/border pieces between the rows and at the top and bottom. Press.

4. Sew 3 of the remaining solid rectangles 2¾" × 12½" to 2 white squares 2¾" × 2¾" for each of the top and bottom borders. Add white rectangles 2¾" × 5" to each end. Sew the borders to the quilt. Press.

5. Layer, quilt, and bind the quilt (pages 116–121).

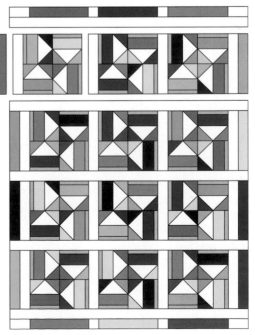

Quilt assembly diagram

SEPTEMBER | OCTOBER

NOVEMBER | DECEMBER

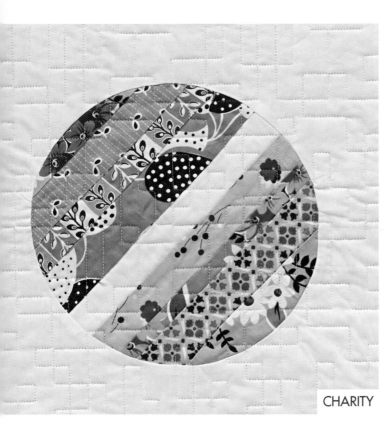
CHARITY

Intermediate Blocks

MASTERING BLOCK-IN-BLOCK DESIGNS, TINY PIECING, AND CURVES

Do you shy away from quilt blocks that look difficult? In this section, you'll build upon your skills with five more quilt designs to keep you on your toes. Grow your quilting techniques beyond the basics with advanced piecing and curves as you incorporate block-in-block designs and tiny piecing. Explore foundation quilting with freezer paper, an unexpected design tool. Whether you're sewing alone or with a bee, you can learn how to gracefully piece circles and arcs into your quilts. Give it a try!

SEPTEMBER
Trellis Crossroads

Made by Jessica Kelly and quilted by Kathie Hudak • Fabric: Bespoken by Pat Bravo, Art Gallery Fabrics

Jessica's quilt is made with symmetrical blocks that resemble a garden trellis when joined. Vibrant colors, floral prints, and a crisp white background provide the perfect pop of brightness. Learn to piece this spin on string blocks and have fun mixing and matching the prints in a collection. Or choose assorted fabrics from your stash for a scrappy look.

Block size: 13″ × 13″ unfinished, 12½″ × 12½″ finished

MATERIALS

- **Prints:** 1 fat quarter in each of 20 different prints for blocks
- **White:** 3 yards for blocks
- **Binding:** ⅝ yard
- **Backing:** 4¾ yards
- **Batting:** 70″ × 83″

CUTTING INSTRUCTIONS

WOF = width of fabric

Prints:

- Cut each fat quarter into 4 strips 5″ × 18″. Subcut each strip into 6 rectangles 2¾″ × 5″ (24 total). Give each bee member 16 rectangles to make 1 block. For the entire quilt, make 30 blocks (480 rectangles total).

White:

- Cut 15 strips 4¾″ × WOF. Subcut each strip into 8 squares 4¾″ × 4¾″ (120 total).

- Cut 30 strips 1″ × WOF. Subcut each strip into 4 strips 1″ × 9¾″ (120 total).

- Give each bee member 4 squares and 4 strips to make 1 block. For the entire quilt, make 30 blocks (120 strips and 120 squares total).

Binding:

- Cut 8 strips 2½″ × WOF.

September | Trellis Crossroads | 79

Block Assembly

1. Pinning along the 5″ sides, join 4 of the 2¾″ × 5″ rectangles with right sides facing. Stitch together and then press the seams open. The pieced strip should measure 5″ × 9½″. Repeat with the other rectangles to piece a total of 4 units.

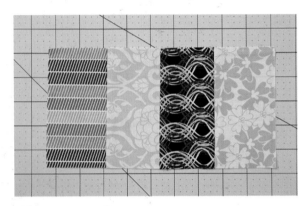

2. Cut each pieced unit in half lengthwise to make 2 pieces, each measuring 2½″ × 9½″.

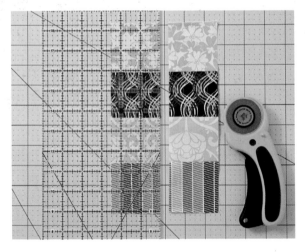

3. Mix and regroup the strips into pairs so the same prints do not touch. Place a white strip 1″ × 9¾″ between each pieced pair. The strip should be about ⅛″ longer than the pieced strips on either end. With the right sides together, stitch the pieced sections to either side of the white strip. Repeat to make 4 units.

4. Cut a 4¾″ white square in half diagonally to make 2 triangles. Repeat with 3 other squares to make 8 triangles total.

5. Fold each triangle in half along the longest edge and use your fingernail to mark a short crease in the center of each. Unfold. Center the marked fold between the second and third pieced rectangles on a side of a pieced unit. Stitch with right sides together. Repeat with other triangles and pieced units.

6. Align the 45° mark on the ruler with the center of the white strip. Trim each of the 4 units to 6¾″ square.

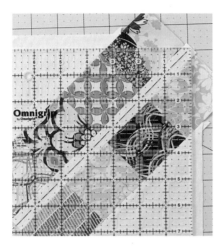

7. Sew together all 4 units so that the white triangles meet in the middle and the white strips form the outline of a diamond shape.

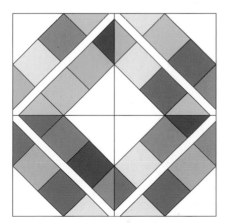

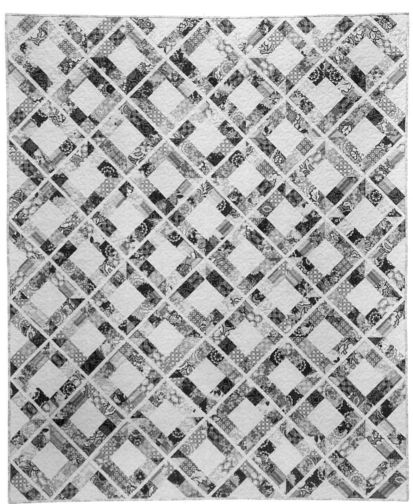

Finished size: 62½″ × 75″

Quilt Construction

Refer to the quilt photo (page 81) and to the quilt assembly diagram (at right).

1. Arrange 30 blocks into 6 rows of 5 blocks each.

2. Sew the blocks into rows. Press.

3. Join the rows. Press.

4. Layer, quilt, and bind the quilt (pages 116–121).

Quilt assembly diagram

Precut squares, strips, and fat quarters

Quilting Fabric Cuts and Collections

When buying quilting fabric, you have the option to mix and match prints and colors for endless possibilities. You can also buy fabric that is part of the same collection, which is a specially designed group of fabrics from a designer. Fabric collections are often available in precut bundles, which come in different sizes. Quilters can save time and money with bundles while also sampling all of the prints in a collection without buying large cuts.

Here are some of the more common cuts of fabric available for quilting. In addition to offering designer collections, many local and online fabric shops sell custom fabric bundles of coordinating prints. Though these fabrics may be from different designers, they share common elements that can help take the guesswork out of combining fabrics!

PRECUT SQUARES
Charm squares measure 5″ × 5″, and a charm pack typically has 20 to 50 squares from the same collection, with or without repeats. *Mosaic Tiles* (page 32) would work well using a charm pack. With 10″ × 10″ fabric squares, precuts such as Moda Layer Cakes are the equivalent of four charm packs in one. These larger squares allow quilters more design possibilities than charm packs.

PRECUT STRIPS
Fabric companies often sell precut strips in a bundle, representing all prints from a collection. These 2½″ strips are cut the width of the fabric and are often known by the names given to them by their manufacturers, such as FreeSpirit Design Rolls, Robert Kaufman Roll-Ups, or Moda Jelly Rolls. Precut strips lend themselves to quick and easy projects. *Bluebell's Cabin* (page 43) is ideal for precut strips. Quilters have even been known to compete in races to see who can piece a roll of fabric strips into a quilt top the quickest.

FAT-QUARTER BUNDLES
A regular ¼ yard of fabric is cut at 9″ × 44″; a fat quarter is twice the length (18″) and half the width (22″). A fat-quarter bundle is made of several 18″ × 22″ cuts of fabric, enough fabric to make a number of quilt patterns in this book, such as *Playing Cards* (page 38), *Neon Ninja Star* (page 71), and *String Circles* (page 104). From a bundle of 10 to 15 fat quarters, you can generally make a crib-size quilt. With 50 to 65 fat quarters, you could probably make a king-size quilt, depending on the pattern you choose.

FAT-EIGHTH AND HALF-YARD BUNDLES
Less common than fat-quarter bundles, fat-eighth bundles contain 9″ × 22″ cuts of fabric from a collection and can be a bargain compared with fat-quarter bundles and sometimes even Layer Cakes. A regular ⅛-yard cut of fabric is 4½″ × 44″. *Triple Star* (page 98) is a great pattern for using fat eighths. A half-yard bundle provides a generous 18″ × 44″ cut of each print. Half-yard bundles are a good choice for favorite collections and for quilters who want to make more than one project with a line of fabric. *Baseball Curves* (page 90) could be completed with half-yard cuts.

OCTOBER
Ziggy Stardust

Made by Colleen Molen • Fabric: Oval Elements by Pat Bravo, Art Gallery Fabrics

Minimalism is a distinction of many modern quilts, and much of that comes through embracing negative space in the design. With its tiny piecing and bold use of white space, this block challenges the quilter to piece triangles, diamonds, and rectangles on a much smaller scale. In Colleen's finished quilt, the blocks are rotated for a geometric twist on a starry sky.

Block size: 12½" × 12½" unfinished, 12" × 12" finished

MATERIALS

- **Solid:** 4¼ yards for blocks

- **Pink dot:** ¾ yard for blocks

- **Green dot:** ¾ yard for blocks

- **Binding:** ⅝ yard

- **Backing:** 4 yards

- **Batting:** 68" × 68"

CUTTING INSTRUCTIONS

WOF = width of fabric

For each bee member, cut enough solid, pink dot, and green dot fabric to make 2 blocks, 1 of each color. You will need to make 1 extra block.

Solid:

- For each bee member, cut the following pieces:

    2 rectangles 5½" × 13" (24 total)

    4 rectangles 2" × 13" (48 total)

    2 rectangles 2" × 4½" (24 total)

    2 rectangles 4½" × 7½" (24 total)

    2 squares 3" × 3" (24 total)

    24 squares 1½" × 1½" (288 total)

Pink dot:

- For each bee member, cut the following pieces:

    1 rectangle 1¼" × 13" (12 total)

    4 rectangles 1½" × 2½" (48 total)

    1 square 3" × 3" (12 total)

Green dot:

- For each bee member, cut the following pieces:

  1 rectangle 1¼″ × 13″ (12 total)

  4 rectangles 1½″ × 2½″ (48 total)

  1 square 3″ × 3″ (12 total)

Binding:

- Cut 7 strips 2½″ × WOF.

Block Assembly

1. To make the diamond units, use a ruler and pencil or Hera marker to mark a diagonal line on 2 solid squares 1½″ × 1½″. With right sides facing, place a square on top of a dot rectangle 1½″ × 2½″ as shown. Sew on the line.

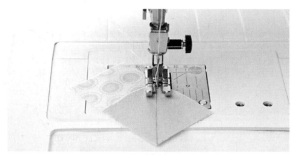

Stitch square to rectangle.

2. Trim the seam allowance to ¼″ and press toward the solid.

3. Place the other marked solid square on top of the other end of the rectangle as shown. Sew on the line.

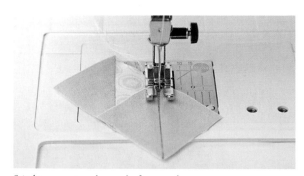

Stitch square to other end of rectangle.

4. Trim the seam allowance to ¼″ and press toward the solid.

5. Repeat Steps 1–4 using 6 solid squares 1½″ × 1½″ and 3 dot rectangles 1½″ × 2½″ to make 4 diamond units for a block.

6. To make half-square triangle units, place a solid square 3″ × 3″ and a dot square 3″ × 3″ right sides together. Sew a scant ¼″ seam around the perimeter, joining the squares.

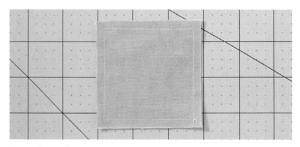

Sew edges of squares.

7. Using a rotary cutter, cut twice diagonally to make 4 half-square triangle units.

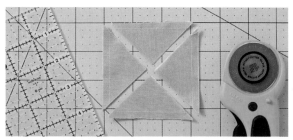

Cut twice diagonally.

8. Press the seams toward the dot fabric. Trim each half-square triangle unit to 1½″ × 1½″, using a clear ruler with a 45° mark to line up with the diagonal seam.

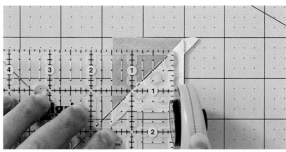

Trim half-square triangle unit.

9. Sew a solid 1½″ square to each of the half-square triangles as shown. Press toward the solid.

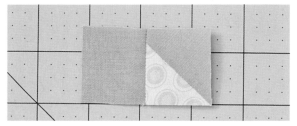

Stitch squares to half-square triangles.

10. Sew a half-square triangle unit to each diamond unit as shown. Press the seams open.

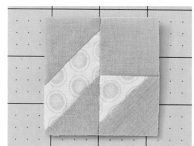

Stitch half-square triangles to diamonds.

Finished size: 60″ × 60″

11. Align 2 units from Step 10 so that the points of the 2 diamonds touch. Sew together. Repeat with 2 more units. Press seams open.

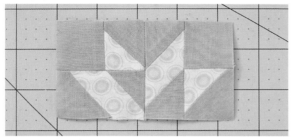

Join units as shown.

12. Sew the 2 units from Step 11 together to complete the diamond star.

13. Sew the solid 2″ × 4½″ rectangle to the top of the star block. Sew the solid 4½″ × 7½″ rectangle to the bottom of the star block. Press toward the solid.

14. Sew the block together in the following order from left to right:

2″ × 13″ solid

4½″ × 13″ star unit

5½″ × 13″ solid

1¼″ × 13″ dot

2″ × 13″ solid

15. Trim the block to 12½″ × 12½″.

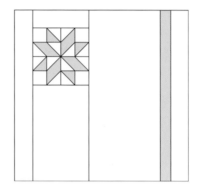

Quilt Construction

Refer to the quilt photo (page 87) and to the quilt assembly diagram (at right).

1. Arrange 25 blocks into 5 rows of 5 blocks each. Turn the blocks as shown in the quilt assembly diagram.

2. Sew the blocks into rows. Press.

3. Join the rows. Press.

4. Layer, quilt, and bind the quilt (pages 116–121).

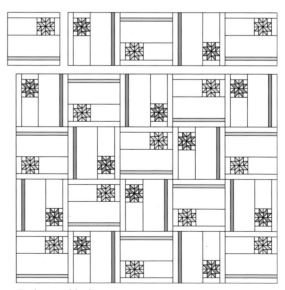

Quilt assembly diagram

The Feel of Fabric

As convenient as it is to shop for fabric online, it often helps to feel a fabric before buying it. Cotton quilting fabrics vary greatly in their *hand*, or how they feel when touched.

When touching a fabric, is it soft or crisp? Does it feel dry or silky to the touch? Though everyone has a preference, a *good hand* generally means that a fabric holds its shape without feeling stiff. The fabric Colleen chose for this quilt is manufactured by Art Gallery, known for silky quilting fabrics in vibrant colors.

The weight of the fabric is also a consideration. While most quilting fabric is medium weight and suitable for patchwork, lightweight fabrics such as voile and heavyweight fabrics such as Japanese linen or even upcycled denim also can be used in patchwork. When pressed, they may be more difficult to work with, depending on how they hold their shape.

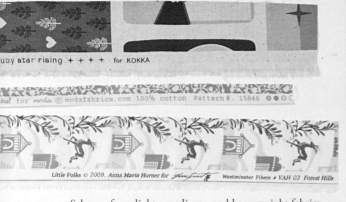

Selvages from light-, medium-, and heavyweight fabrics

Comparing Thread

Thread also can be described as light- or heavyweight, but is most often identified by its purpose. Is the thread for hand sewing, machine sewing, or quilting? Unless you plan to quilt a project by hand, you should generally look for a good-quality cotton or polyester thread that is made for machine sewing. All-purpose thread is a good choice for most projects.

When choosing a thread color for piecing and quilting, match the color to the sashing or background fabric, or choose a shade featured prominently in the blocks. Stock up on white thread, which is a great choice for many quilt projects.

Baseball Curves

Made by Lindsay Conner and quilted by Angela Walters   •   Fabric: Designer Solids, FreeSpirit Fabrics

Sewing precise curves is not as scary as it seems, especially with the perfect cutting template. Although the pinning and fabric piecing is different, sewing curves is not that different from sewing in a straight line after you have gotten some practice. The Baseball Curves block is a modern take on the traditional Drunkard's Trail, also called Friendship Circle. With multicolored background fabrics that light up like a disco floor, the quilt's curves roll gently like waves across each block. Make the layout your own by twisting selected blocks for endless design possibilities.

Block size: 13″ × 13″ unfinished, 12½″ × 12½″ finished

MATERIALS

- **Solids:** ⅜ yard each of 12 different colors for blocks

- **White:** 2⅔ yards for blocks

- **Binding:** ¾ yard
- **Batting:** 83″ × 83″

- **Backing:** 7 yards
- **Template material**

CUTTING INSTRUCTIONS

WOF = width of fabric

Make templates, using the patterns on pages 95–97.

Solids:

- Fold the solid-colored fabrics into equal thirds across the width of the fabric. Position template A and 2 of template C on the fabric stack and cut through all layers. From each fabric, cut 3 of A (36 total) and 6 of C (72 total) for each bee member to complete 3 blocks.

White:

- Fold the fabric into equal thirds across the width of the fabric. Position template B on the fabric stack and cut through all layers. Cut 6 of B (72 total) for each bee member.

Binding:

- Cut 9 strips 2½″ × WOF.

Block Assembly

1. Fold the block center (A) in half so the short ends are touching and finger-press to mark the center line. Repeat with each white arc (B) and outer curve (C), folding in half to mark the center of each piece.

2. Matching up the folded center lines, pin together the block center and the white arc with a single pin. Align the pieces and pin them together at each end with a single pin; follow the fabric's natural curve to secure each seam with several more pins.

3. Use a scant ¼" seam allowance to stitch along the pinned seams, removing the pins as you go. Press the seams toward the solid fabric.

4. Pin and attach the outer curve to the white arc you just attached. Repeat to stitch the arc and the outer curve to the opposite side.

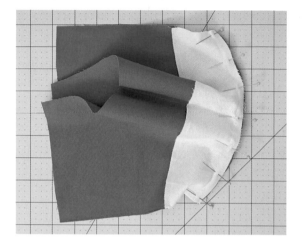

5. Clip the inner curves and notch the outer curves, making sure not to cut too close to the stitching line. Press and trim the block to 13" × 13" square.

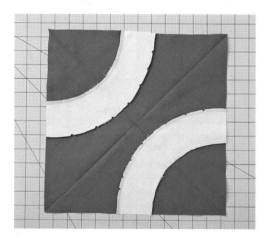

Quilt Construction

Refer to the quilt photo (below) and to the quilt assembly diagram (at right).

1. Arrange 36 blocks into 6 rows of 6 blocks each, so that no blocks of the same color touch. Use the edges of the white arc to align the blocks, and then pin the blocks with right sides together.

2. Sew the blocks into rows. Press.

3. Join the rows. Press.

4. Layer, quilt, and bind the quilt (pages 116–121).

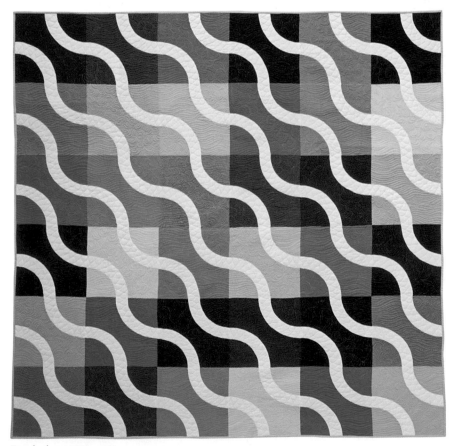

Quilt assembly diagram

Finished size: 75″ × 75″

Curved Piecing

For smooth pieced curves, pin outward from the center and use a pin or your fingers to carefully guide the fabric through the machine along the curve, making sure not to introduce any wrinkles. Position one hand near the presser foot and one hand between the fabric layers being sewn together for extra control. After sewing the curve, stitch over any uneven stitches in a second pass.

Clip and notch the inner and outer curves to help curved fabric fit together. Inner curves, which look like smiles, are clipped with tiny, straight snips of the scissors. Outer curves, which look like rolling hills, are notched with tiny V-shaped sections. Make sure not to cut too close to the stitching line while clipping and notching the curves.

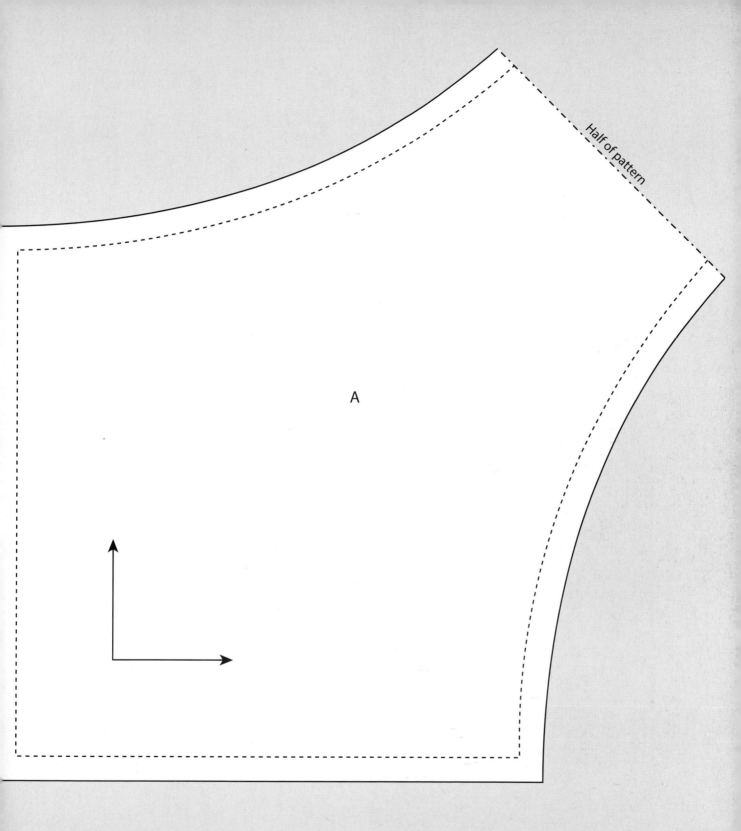

Half of pattern

A

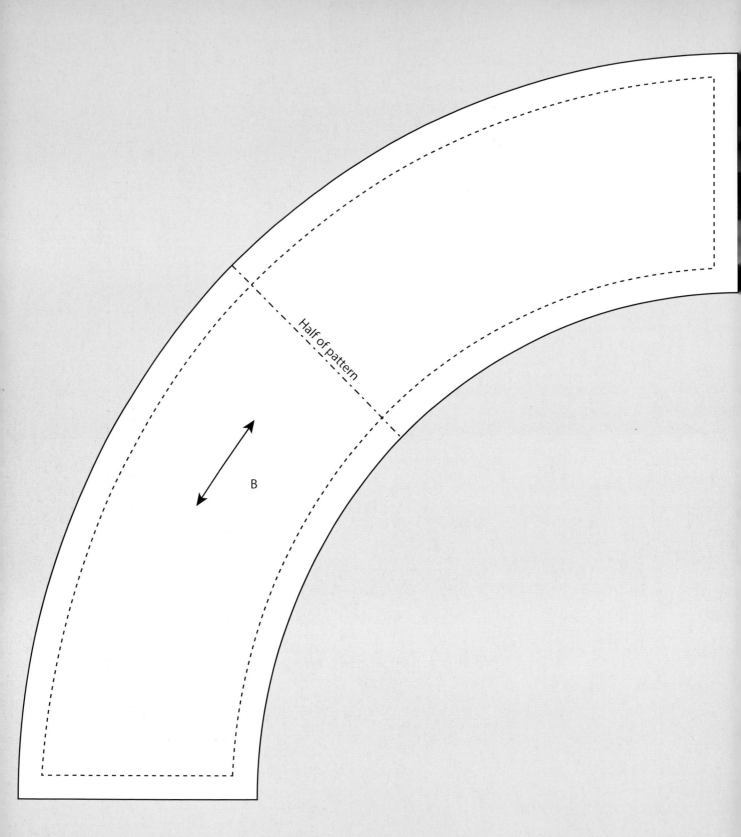

Half of pattern

B

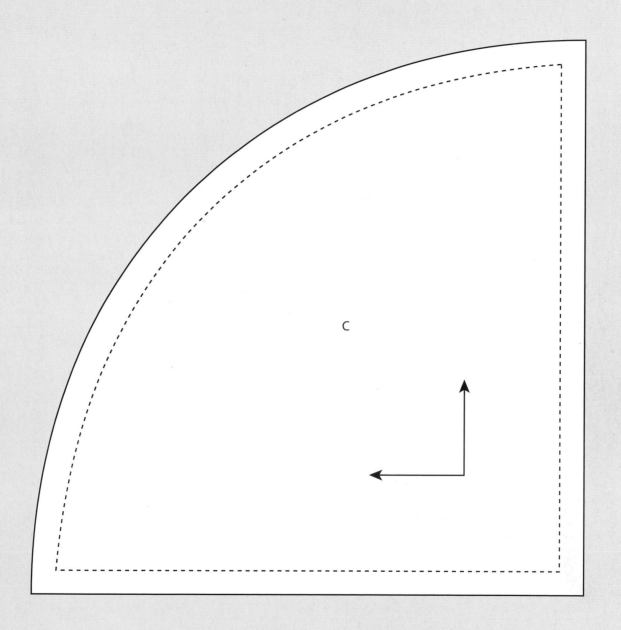

C

Triple Star

Made by Elena Roscoe and quilted by Angela Walters • Fabric: assorted scraps and Flea Market Fancy by Denyse Schmidt, FreeSpirit Fabrics

Block-in-block construction is not as tricky as it looks, even with the smallest of shapes nestled inside larger ones. Elena's Triple Star block is a variation of the traditional Rising Star, but with one extra layer. Each scrappy block features two complementary colors, and the finished stars are sashed in white to allow the eye to hone in on the colorful, vibrant prints in each one. Use this pattern to make Triple Star pillows or piece a quilt that's totally custom, made from stars of different sizes.

Block size: 16½" × 16½" unfinished, 16" × 16" finished

MATERIALS

- **Prints:** 2¼ yards total, using a variety of scraps, charm squares, or fat quarters for blocks
- **White:** 5 yards for blocks, sashing, and borders
- **Pink print:** ⅞ yard for border
- **Binding:** ¾ yard
- **Backing:** 5¼ yards
- **Batting:** 74" × 92"

CUTTING INSTRUCTIONS

WOF = width of fabric

For a color pairing like the one in Elena's quilt, choose 2 specific colors for each quilter's block kit and pick a variety of prints in each color.

Prints:

- For fussy-cut centers, cut 12 squares 2½" × 2½" and give a square to each bee member.

- Cut 48 squares 2½" × 2½" and 48 squares 3½" × 3½", and give 4 of each size (2 of each color) to each bee member.

- Cut 48 squares 5½" × 5½" and give 4 (2 of each color) to each bee member.

White:

- For each bee member, cut the following pieces:

    4 squares 1½" × 1½" (48 total)

    8 squares 2½" × 2½" (96 total)

    4 squares 3½" × 3½" (48 total)

    4 squares 4½" × 4½" (48 total)

    4 squares 5½" × 5½" (48 total)

White, continued:

- For sashing and borders, cut 22 strips 2½" × WOF, joining as needed to piece longer strips. From these strips, cut the following pieces:

   8 strips 2½" × 16½" for sashing between blocks

   3 strips 2½" × 52½" for sashing between rows

   2 strips 2½" × 56½" for top and bottom inner borders

   2 strips 2½" × 70½" for side inner borders

   2 strips 2½" × 80½" for side outer borders

   2 strips 2½" × 66½" for top and bottom outer borders

Pink print:

- Cut 7 strips 3½" × WOF. Join and trim to make 2 strips 3½" × 62½" for top and bottom borders and 2 strips 3½" × 74½" for side borders.

Binding:

- Cut 8 strips 2½" × WOF.

Block Assembly

1. To make the half-square triangle units, place a white square 2½" × 2½" on top of a print square 2½" × 2½" with right sides together. With a ruler and pencil or Hera marker, mark a diagonal line across the top square.

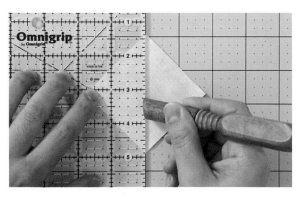

2. Sew ¼" from the marked line on both sides.

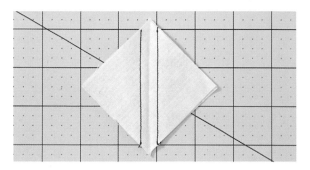

3. Cut on the marked line.

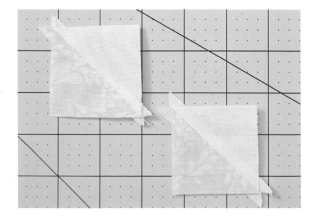

4. Press the seams open. Trim to 1½″ × 1½″, using a clear ruler with a 45° mark to line up with the diagonal seam. Repeat with 3 additional pairs of 2½″ print and white squares.

5. Arrange the inner star with the fussy-cut print in the center. Arrange the half-square triangles so a unit of each color is on each side of the square. Place the 1½″ white squares in the corners.

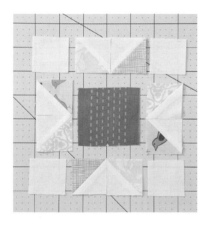

6. Sew together each pair of half-square triangles with right sides facing. Press seams open. Stitch the left and right star points to the center. Stitch the solid corners to the loose star points, and then attach to the top and bottom of the block. This completed star now becomes the center block for the next star.

Finished size: 66″ × 84″

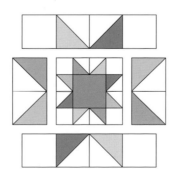

7. Pair the 3½″ print and white squares together. Mark a diagonal line, sew, and cut as described above. Trim to 2½″ × 2½″.

8. Pair the 5½″ print and white squares together. Mark a diagonal line, sew, and cut as described above. Trim to 4½″ × 4½″.

9. Arrange and sew the pieces together, treating each completed star as the new center.

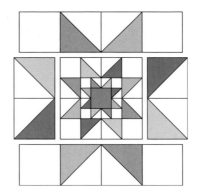

Quilt Construction

Refer to the quilt photo (page 101) and to the quilt assembly diagram (at right).

1. Arrange 12 blocks into 4 rows of 3 blocks each. Add the 2½″ × 16½″ sashing pieces between the blocks in each row. Press.

2. Sew the rows of blocks to the 2½″ × 52½″ sashing pieces. Press.

3. Add inner white side borders. Press. Add inner white top and bottom borders. Press.

4. Add pink side borders. Press. Add pink top and bottom borders. Press.

5. Add outer white side borders. Press. Add outer white top and bottom borders. Press.

6. Layer, quilt, and bind the quilt (pages 116–121).

Quilt assembly diagram

Fussy Cutting

The center of each Triple Star block features a sewing notion, such as scissors or thread. Elena used the technique of *fussy cutting*, which is centering a specific print inside of a specific cut of fabric. You'll need a clear ruler or a template and a rotary cutter for fussy cutting. Remember that the fussy-cut square will lose ¼" on each side during block construction, so choose a print that will not be cut off around the edges.

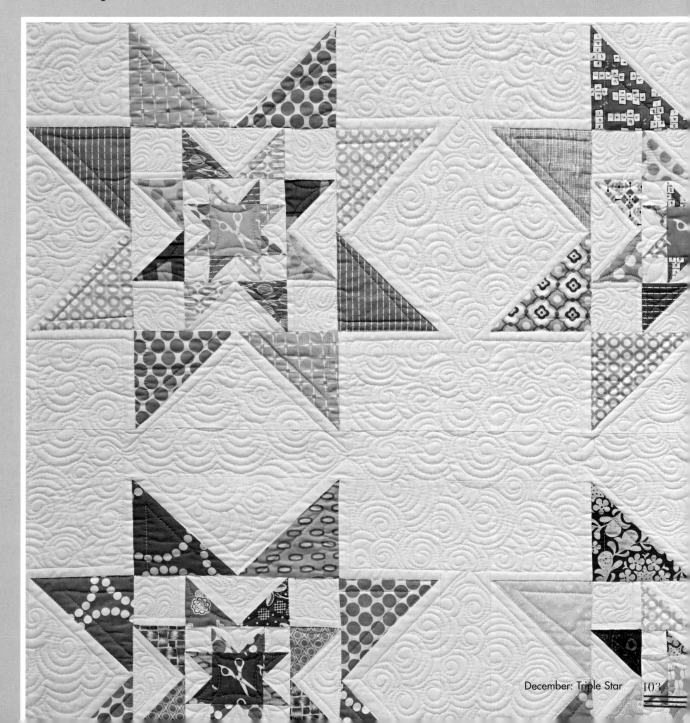

String Circles

Made by Lindsay Conner and quilted by Quilting by the Stitch • Fabric: Flea Market Fancy
by Denyse Schmidt, FreeSpirit Fabrics

This foundation-pieced block features a circle of strips pieced inside background fabric. String blocks differ from other types of quilt blocks in that fabric is sewn onto a foundation of paper or fabric. And if you're not sure about the pieced circle, you can simplify this pattern by substituting raw-edge appliqué. But don't shy away from the pieced circle before giving it a try. The blocks in this quilt were made by fourteen quilters, many of them new to sewing curves. Knowing the quilt was for charity encouraged them to try something new. These instructions are for a bee of twelve people.

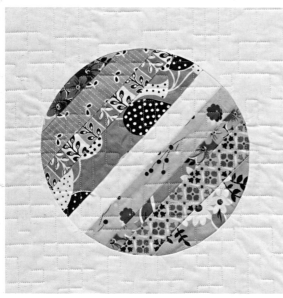

Block size: 12½″ × 12½″ unfinished, 12″ × 12″ finished

MATERIALS

- **Prints:** ¼ yard (or 1 fat quarter) each of 16 prints for blocks

- **White:** 4 yards (5¼ yards if fabric is less than 42″ wide) for background

- **Binding:** ⅝ yard

- **Backing:** 4 yards

- **Batting:** 68″ × 68″

- **Freezer paper**

- **Gluestick**

CUTTING INSTRUCTIONS

WOF = width of fabric

Make templates, using the patterns on page 111 or using a circle cutter.

Freezer paper:

- Cut 25 circles 8¾″ diameter, and give 2 to each bee member. (The host or other chosen bee member will make 3 blocks.)

Prints:

- Cut into strips in varying widths of 1″–2″ across the width of the fabrics. Trim the strips to 9″ long until you have 250 strips, and give each bee member 20 strips in various prints.

White:

- Cut fabric into strips 14″ × WOF and subcut into 14″ × 14″ squares (25 total). Give 2 squares to each bee member (3 to the host).

  From leftover yardage, cut 2 strips 1½″ × 9″ for each bee member (give 3 to the host for 25 total).

- *To make background for pieced circle:* Fold squares in half lengthwise, then widthwise, and press. Use a template or a circle cutter to cut a circle that is 7¾″ in diameter. If using a circle cutter, center the compass point on the tip of the folded corner (center point of fabric), and cut a quarter-circle from folded fabric. (Refer to Cutting Circles, page 110.)

Binding:

- Cut 7 strips 2½″ × WOF.

Block Assembly

1. Fold the circle of freezer paper in half. Open and use a gluestick to position the white fabric strip along the center line of the freezer paper's shiny side.

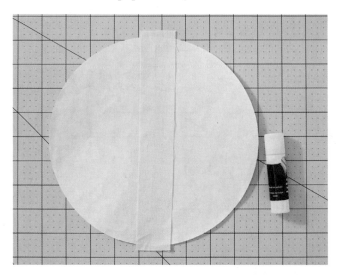

2. Choose a print fabric strip. With the right sides of the fabrics together, stitch the strip to the side of the glued center strip, using a scant ¼″ seam allowance. Open the strip to the side and finger-press the seam flat.

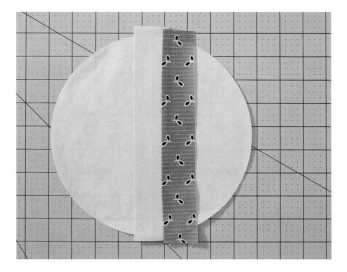

3. Add strips to left and right sides of the center strip until the entire freezer-paper template is covered. Press the circle with an iron to temporarily adhere the fabric to the freezer-paper template.

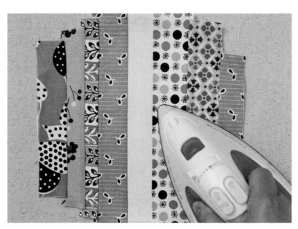

4. Trim the excess fabric away from the circle but leave the paper attached for now.

5. With the right sides facing up, center the strip-pieced circle on top of the background fabric with the circle cutout. Use a ruler to make sure the center strip is aligned on a diagonal.

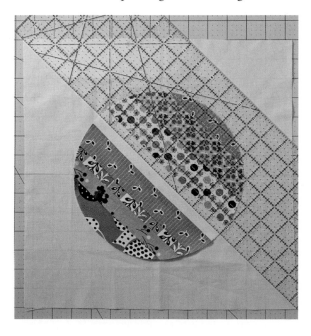

6. To piece the circle into the background, fold the outer edges of the background piece over the circle. With right sides together, align the raw edges and pin at the bottom.

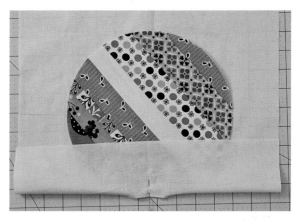

7. Repeat and pin at the top, left, and right.

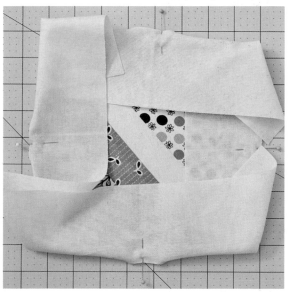

8. Add pins halfway between each of these anchor points, following the circle's natural curve. Continue to add pins until the background is pinned all the way around the circle.

9. With the background fabric on top, stitch around the perimeter, removing pins as you sew. Use your hands to smooth out any potential wrinkles as they come under the presser foot.

10. Remove the freezer paper. With a square ruler, trim the block to 12½″ × 12½″, making sure to remove equal amounts from each side. The circle should remain centered and the diagonal center line should still rest on the ruler's 45° mark.

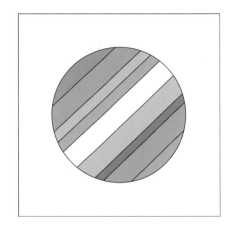

Quilt Construction

Refer to the quilt photo (next page) and to the quilt assembly diagram (at right).

1. Arrange 25 blocks into 5 rows of 5 blocks each.

2. Sew the blocks into rows. Press.

3. Join the rows. Press.

4. Layer, quilt, and bind the quilt (pages 116–121).

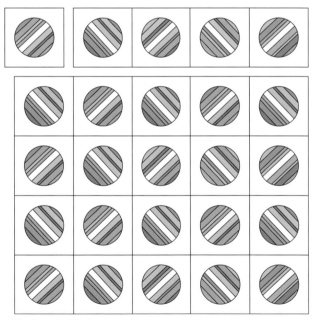

Quilt assembly diagram

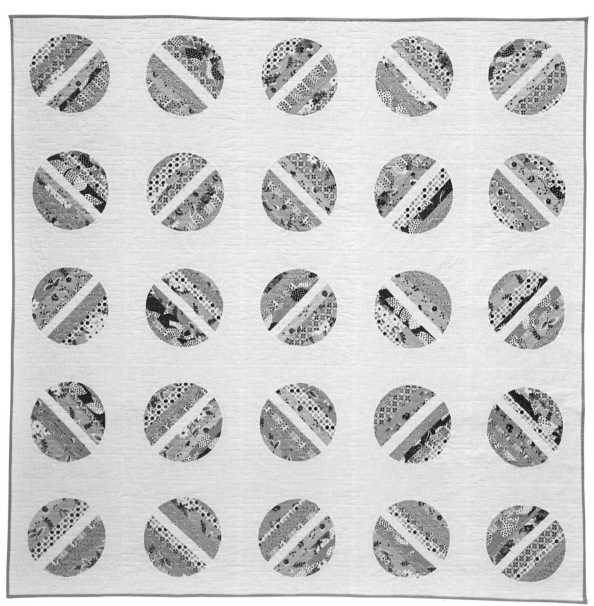

Finished size: 60″ × 60″

Variation: Raw-Edge Appliqué

To skip the curved piecing and complete this quilt using raw-edge appliqué, cut the background fabric to 13″ × 13″ and leave it whole—do not cut a circle out of the fabric. Remove the freezer paper from the pieced circle. Use a gluestick or spray adhesive to temporarily adhere the circle to the center of the background fabric, pinning as needed. Use a zigzag stitch around the perimeter of the circle to attach it to the background block. Trim the block to 12½″ × 12½″.

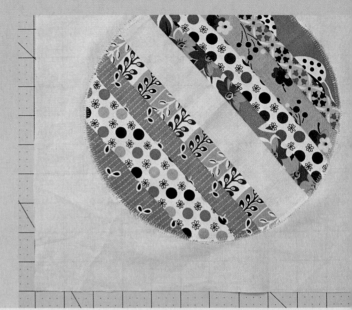

Foundation Blocks

Freezer paper, available in many grocery stores, makes a great foundation for string blocks. Fabric can be temporarily adhered to the shiny side of the paper with an iron. For easier removal of the freezer paper from the finished block, shorten your machine's normal stitch length by one or two settings before you sew. This creates a perforated line effect! If you shorten the stitch length to the lowest setting, the paper may fall off before you're ready to remove it.

If freezer paper is not available, regular computer paper will work in a pinch.

Cutting Circles

When you're cutting multiple circles from freezer paper and fabric, a rotary circle cutter comes in handy. To cut a circle from the center point of a fabric square, fold the fabric in quarters and press. Then align the circle cutter like a compass on the folded corner.

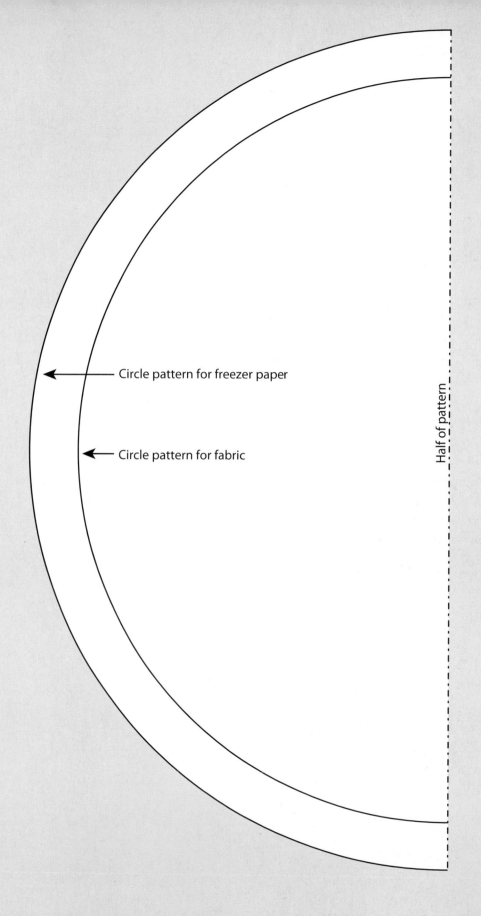

Circle pattern for freezer paper

Circle pattern for fabric

Half of pattern

Finishing

Blocks, Borders, and Sashing

When completing a quilt top, your arrangement may include only blocks or a combination of blocks and sashing (the fabric mortar between blocks) and an outer border. When adding a border to a quilt top, sew on the side borders first. You can find the measurement for the side borders by taking a tape measure through the vertical center of the quilt top.

To attach border strips, place a pin at the centers of the side border strips. Then pin these to the centers of the sides of the quilt top. Stitch the side borders and press. Measure horizontally across the center of the quilt top to get the top and bottom border measurements. Repeat the process to attach border strips to the top and bottom of the quilt. If you do not have enough continuous yardage for the border strips, piece together shorter strips and center the seams on the quilt top.

Backing

The back of a quilt can be a coordinating print, a solid, or a mixture of the two. It is often necessary to piece fabric together to make a quilt back, so many quilters use this as a chance to show a patchwork design made of large strips, squares, or other shapes. A quilt back should be 2″–4″ larger than the quilt top on each side, with the excess fabric trimmed after quilting.

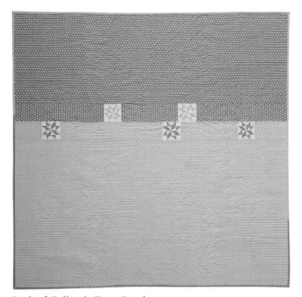

Back of Colleen's *Ziggy Stardust*

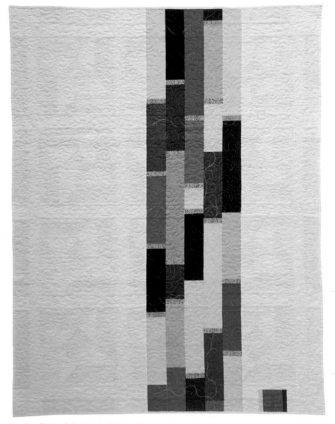

Back of Cindy's *Neon Ninja Star*

Back of *String Circles*, the charity quilt

Whether borne out of necessity, creativity, or a little bit of both, pieced quilt backs offer a chance to have fun with design. Cindy used leftover fabrics from the quilt front to create an interesting pieced quilt back. Colleen made patchwork stars to create a simpler version of the design on the front of her quilt. I backed my quilts with large cuts of coordinating fabrics.

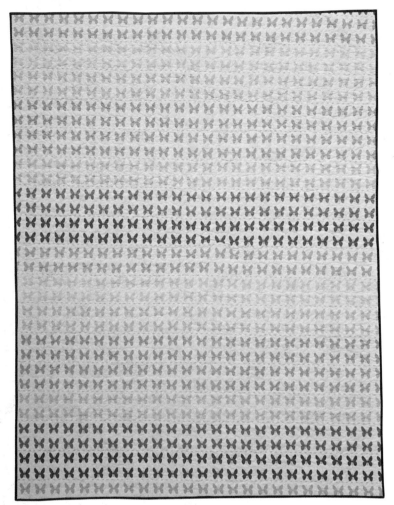

Vintage sheets, such as Jeni's, can make great quilt backs. They are often large enough to back the quilt top without piecing, but they are loose and soft enough to be easier to quilt than a new, tightly woven sheet. Because most quilting fabrics are 45″ wide at most, piecing two or more fabrics together is necessary for most quilt backs crib size or larger.

Elena asked bee members to write their names on small signature blocks to be included on the quilt back. This is a great way to remember your friends from the bee. It also comes in handy if you give the quilt as a gift or donate it to a charity—it's great to recognize the helping hands that went into making a quilt.

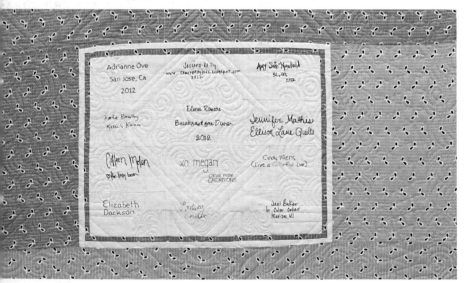

Quilt Sizes and Batting

When shopping for batting, keep in mind the size of the quilt top and add 2″–4″ to each side, just like with the quilt back. For the quilt patterns in this book, we recommend adding 4″ to each side. The type of batting is up to you, but many quilters prefer low-loft cotton batting (which gives washed quilts a crinkly look) or a polyester or poly/cotton blend (for a less crinkly texture). Batting can be purchased by the yard or in prepackaged cuts in common bedding sizes. Scraps of leftover batting can be pieced together with fusible web or thread. Actual measurements may vary, but common packaged batting sizes are as follows:

CRIB: 45″ × 60″

TWIN: 72″ × 90″

FULL/DOUBLE: 81″ × 96″

QUEEN: 90″ × 108″

KING: 120″ × 120″

Join scraps of batting with fusible web.

The Quilt Sandwich and Basting

To get ready for quilt assembly, make the basic *quilt sandwich*, which consists of three layers: the backing, the batting, and the quilt top. The wrong sides of both the backing and the quilt top should directly touch the batting in the middle.

Basting a quilt top is the process of temporarily adhering these three layers together in preparation for quilting. If you plan to send the quilt to a longarm quilter, you will not need to baste it. You can baste a quilt with safety pins (curved pins for quilt basting are ideal), loose and long hand stitches, spray adhesive, or a combination of these methods. For instance, for larger quilts, I often spray baste and then secure the layers with safety pins, so the fabrics aren't likely to shift during quilting.

To get a smooth finish while basting a quilt, spread the backing wrong side up on the floor and tape the edges down with masking tape. T-pins can be used to secure the backing to carpeted floors. Center the batting on top, and place the quilt top right side up on top of the batting and backing. Make sure all layers are centered and smooth out the wrinkles with an iron.

TO BASTE WITH PINS (good for machine quilting)   Place a safety pin every 3″ to 4″ through all three layers of the quilt sandwich. Begin in the center and move out toward the edges, smoothing out the wrinkles as you go.

TO BASTE WITH THREAD (ideal for hand quilting)   Use a long needle and thread that is visible against the quilt top, and sew long stitches approximately the length of the needle through all three layers. Start in the center and move outward, smoothing out any wrinkles.

TO BASTE WITH SPRAY ADHESIVE (good for all types of quilting)   Prepare the quilt sandwich as before, but leave off the quilt top. Pick up one corner or edge of the batting and use spray adhesive between the backing and batting. Press the batting down and smooth out any wrinkles. Move to the other end of the quilt sandwich and spray a bit at a time from one end to the other, adhering the batting to the backing. Place the quilt top on the quilt sandwich and repeat the spray basting to adhere the top two layers. It is best to spray baste in a well-ventilated area.

Quilting Styles

Whether you quilt by hand, by machine, or by check (passing it along to a longarm quilter), quilting will enhance the look of a quilt. A few of the quilts in this book are finished by methods such as stitch in-the-ditch (sewing along the seams), straight-line quilting, or free-motion quilting designs such as swirls, loops, or zigzags. For a more detailed look at various quilting designs, study the finished quilts in this book and check out *Free-Motion Quilting with Angela Walters* (from C&T Publishing), *Beginner's Guide to Free-Motion Quilting* by Natalia Bonner (from Stash Books), and *Modern Quilting Designs* by Bethany Pease (from Stash Books).

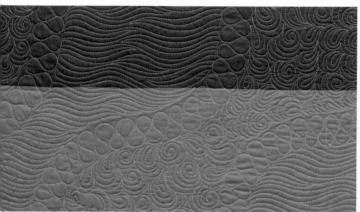

Various styles of free-motion quilting

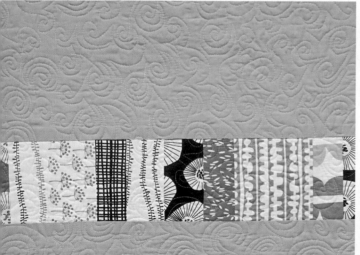

Hand stitching

Binding

The last step of making a quilt is attaching the binding, the narrow fabric sewn around the edge to give it a polished look. Binding strips can be cut along the crosswise grain (width) of fabric, or along the bias (diagonal) for a greater stretch, which is useful for quilts with rounded edges. Binding strips are typically cut 2″–3″ wide, and when joined, they should measure at least 12″ longer than the perimeter of the quilt. The width of binding strips will depend on your preference. Keep in mind that wider binding strips will yield a wider finished binding. The thickness of the batting is another consideration when choosing a binding width. My go-to binding is double-fold straight-grain binding with 2½″ strips, which yields a binding that is less than ½″ wide. Always trim the excess backing and batting from the quilt before attaching the binding.

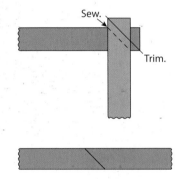

DOUBLE-FOLD STRAIGHT-GRAIN BINDING (FRENCH FOLD)

Cut the binding strips across the width of fabric and piece together with a diagonal seam to make a continuous binding strip. Press the seams open; then use an iron to press the entire strip in half lengthwise with the wrong sides together.

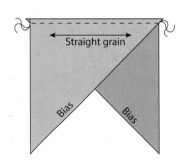

CONTINUOUS BIAS BINDING

Cut the fabric for the bias binding so it is a square. For example, cut ½ yard of fabric to an 18″ square. Cut the square in half diagonally, creating two triangles. Sew these triangles together as shown, pressing the seam open. Using a ruler, mark the parallelogram with lines spaced the width of the bias strips. Cut along the first line about 5″. Join Side 1 and Side 2 to form a tube. Line A will line up with the raw edge at B. This will allow the

first line to be offset by one strip width, creating a continuous bias binding. Pin the raw ends together, making sure that the lines match. Sew with a ¼″ seam allowance. Press seams open. Then cut along the lines.

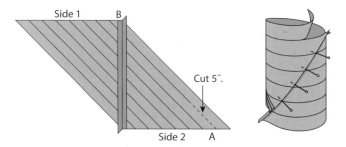

ATTACH BINDING

Pin the raw edges of the binding to the edge of the quilt in the bottom center, and leave the first few inches of the binding unattached. Start sewing, using a ¼″ seam allowance. Stop ¼″ away from the first corner (see Step 1); backstitch one stitch. Lift the presser foot and needle. Rotate the quilt a quarter turn. Fold the binding at a right angle so it extends straight above the quilt (see Step 2). Then bring the binding strip down even with the edge of the quilt (see Step 3). Begin sewing at the folded edge. Repeat for all the corners.

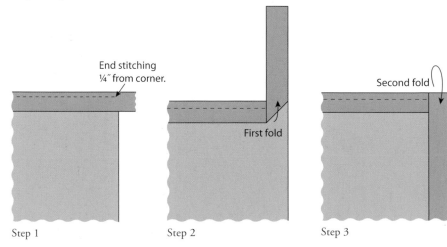

FINISH THE BINDING

There are two basic ways to join the ends of the binding when they meet.

METHOD 1   Fold under the beginning end of the binding strip ¼″. Lay the ending binding strip over the beginning folded end. Continue stitching the seam beyond the folded edge.

METHOD 2   Fold the ending tail of the binding back on itself where it meets the beginning binding tail. From the fold, measure and mark the cut width of the binding strip. Cut the ending binding tail to this measurement. For example, if the binding is cut 2½″ wide, measure from the fold on the ending tail of the binding 2½″ and cut the binding tail to this length. Open both tails. Place one tail on top of the other tail at right angles, right sides together. Mark a diagonal line and stitch on the line. Trim the seam to ¼″. Press open. Finish sewing the binding to the quilt.

After attaching the binding completely to one side of the quilt with one of these methods, trim the excess binding. Fold the binding over the raw edges to the other side of the quilt and hand stitch or machine stitch, mitering the corners.

BY HAND OR BY MACHINE?

While machine-stitched binding is quicker, hand-finished binding shows less visible thread and is the preferred method for quilters looking for a clean and finished look from the front of the quilt.

If you plan to finish the second side of the binding by hand, start by machine-sewing the binding to the *front* of the quilt. Finish the binding by folding it to the back; then use an invisible stitch.

If you plan to machine stitch the entire binding, start by sewing the binding to the *back* of the quilt. Finish the binding by folding it to the front; then machine stitch from the front.

About the Quilters

Photo by Michael Hanna

JENI BAKER (*Stacked Windmills*, page 61) loves to find ways to be creative every day, whether it's through photography, sewing, or quilting! She has been sewing off and on for about ten years. She has recently entered the world of fabric design as a licensed designer for Art Gallery Fabrics. In her spare time, Jeni enjoys collecting vintage kitchenware and spending time with her pet bunny, George. To learn more about Jeni and her quilting adventures, visit her blog In Color Order. (incolororder.com)

Photo by Lindsey Bohr

MEGAN BOHR (*Painter's Palette*, page 48) lives in small-town Iowa where she designs modern quilts. Taught by her grandmother and her mother, Megan started sewing and quilting when she was twelve and never looked back. Now, fourteen years later, she loves to share her modern sewing and quilting and inspire others on her blog, Canoe Ridge Creations. Megan is also the social media coordinator of The Sewing Summit, a modern sewing and blogging conference in Utah. (canoeridgecreations.com)

Photo by Ashley Leath

KATIE BOWLBY (*Cordelia's Garden*, page 66) lives in Alabama with her husband and son. She works as a copy editor for *Southern Living* magazine and loves sewing and quilting in her free time. Her design was inspired by a quilt top made by her great-great-grandmother Cordelia Doust Bourgeois. You can find Katie via her blog, Katie's Korner. (kakorner.blogspot.com)

Photo by Jesse Tendler

ELIZABETH DACKSON (*Come Together*, page 56) is a self-proclaimed fabric addict and modern quilter. She designs quilt patterns found both on her blog, Don't Call Me Betsy, and in various quilting publications including *Quiltmaker*, *International Quilt Festival: Quilt Scene*, *Modern Quilts Unlimited*, *Quilty*, and FatQuarterly.com. An active member of the Tampa Modern Quilt Guild, she released her first quilting book, *Becoming a Confident Quilter*, in the fall of 2013. Elizabeth lives in Florida with her husband, son, and neurotic beagle. (dontcallmebetsy.com)

Photo by Jason Kelly

JESSICA KELLY (*Trellis Crossroads*, page 78) finds design inspiration in everyday life and often captures quilt ideas on napkins or paper scraps before trying them out on fabric. She quilts from her home in Pittsburgh, Pennsylvania, where her supportive husband and two Labrador retrievers turn a blind eye to her ever-growing fabric stash. Jessica's work has appeared in *Quilt* magazine, and she also designs for her pattern store and Moda Bake Shop. Visit her blog at Sew Crafty Jess. (sewcraftyjess.blogspot.com)

Photo by James Mathis

JENNIFER MATHIS (*Playing Cards*, page 38) is a southern mama who fell in love with quilting and sewing in 2010. She taught herself to sew with gusto, jumped right into the online sewing world, and never looked back. With her husband cheering her on, she puts her organizational and teaching skills to use planning Sew South, a modern sewing retreat in Charlotte. Taking care of her family, reading, sketching, and dreaming of new projects keeps her busy, although occasionally she cooks dinner, too. She has been published in *Quilty* magazine and *Modern Quilts from the Blogging Universe*. Learn more about Jennifer at her blog, Ellison Lane Quilts. (ellisonlane.blogspot.com)

Photo by Brad Molen

COLLEEN MOLEN (*Ziggy Stardust*, page 84) is greatly inspired by traditions, antique quilts, and the lives of the women who created them. She loves taking anything old and making it new, using bold patterns and bright colors. She started quilting just a few years ago to make a quilt for her daughter's first birthday, finishing it in time for her second birthday. Living in Utah with her husband and two daughters, Colleen enjoys learning new things about life as she creates a place her family is proud to call home, and she hopes that what she creates will make future generations want to know her. You can find out more about Colleen at her blog, The Busy Bean. (thebusybean.com)

Photo by Brad Newbold

AMY (SUKIE) NEWBOLD (*Mosaic Tiles*, page 32) started quilting in 2010. She was inspired by her mother-in-law, who has been sewing for more than 40 years. Sukie lives with her husband and two kids in Salt Lake City, Utah. By day, she works as an accountant, but she fits in sewing at night and on the weekends. She loves long walks on the beach, challenging herself to finish large-scale sewing projects, and organizing swaps and bees. She also blogs about her creations. (sukiedontyaknow.com)

Photo by Adrianne Ove

ADRIANNE OVE (*Bluebell's Cabin*, page 43) is a quilter and pattern designer who finds inspiration in everyday shapes and colors. She loves taking a simple idea and finding innovative ways to go from simple to modern. Growing up in Santa Cruz, California, she was influenced by a coastal lifestyle and beach themes. Adrianne is an enthusiastic advocate for the Modern Quilt Guild and is active with the online quilting community. You can find Adrianne at her blog, Little Bluebell. (littlebluebell.com)

Photo by Jemma Coleman

ELENA ROSCOE (*Triple Star*, page 98) lives in South Florida with her husband, Michael, and their black lab, Seamus. She began sewing as a little girl when her mother taught her to make clothes for her Barbie dolls. From then on, Elena was hooked on the creative process. She is active in the online sewing community and enjoys interacting with stitch friends from around the globe. Learn more about Elena at her blog, Hot Pink Stitches. (hotpinkstitches.com)

Photo by Christa Wiens

CINDY WIENS (*Neon Ninja Star*, page 71) combines the traditions of her Mennonite Brethren ancestors and her love of beautiful fabrics, especially solids, to design refreshingly colorful quilts. Besides making quilts for friends and family, Cindy has donated quilts to help raise money for disaster relief at an annual auction in her hometown of Fresno, California. Cindy's work has appeared on *Quilting Arts TV* and in *International Quilt Festival: Quilt Scene* and *Modern Patchwork,* and she has published patterns with JWD Publishing. Visit her blog, Live a Colorful Life. (aroundtheblockdesigns.blogspot.com)

About the Author

Photo by Jeremiah Blackford

LINDSAY CONNER (*Baseball Curves*, page 90, and *String Circles*, page 104) is a writer, editor, and quilter living in Nashville, Tennessee, with her husband and two loveable cats, Murph and Chloe. She loves teaching friends to quilt, swapping crafts and fabric with sewists around the globe, and sharing her creative journey with anyone who will listen. In 2011, Lindsay and her crafty partner-in-crime, Mary Jaracz, launched Craft Buds, a space to share handmade business tips and tutorials. Lindsay's work has appeared in *Stitch* and *Stitch Craft Create* magazines and the *One-Yard Wonders* books. She blogs about her crafty ventures at Lindsay Sews (lindsaysews.com) and Craft Buds (craftbuds.com).

Resources

C&T PUBLISHING
ctpub.com

COATS & CLARK
coatsandclark.com

ELECTRIC QUILT SOFTWARE
electricquilt.com

FREESPIRIT FABRICS
freespiritfabric.com

OLFA
olfa.com

PELLON
pellonprojects.com

TIMELESS TREASURES
ttfabrics.com